RAND NATIONAL DEFENSE RESEARCH INSTITUTE

T0288583

A Building Partner Capacity Assessment Framework

Tracking Inputs, Outputs, Outcomes, Disrupters, and Workarounds

Christopher Paul, Brian Gordon, Jennifer D. P. Moroney,

Lisa Saum-Manning, Beth Grill, Colin P. Clarke, Heather Peterson

Prepared for the Joint Staff J5, the Office of Cost Assessment
and Program Evaluation in the Office of the Secretary of Defense,
and the Office of the Under Secretary of Defense for Policy

For more information on this publication, visit www.rand.org/t/rr935

Library of Congress Cataloging-in-Publication Data
ISBN: 9780833088673

Published by the RAND Corporation, Santa Monica, Calif.

© Copyright 2015 RAND Corporation

RAND® is a registered trademark.

Cover image by U.S. Army Europe Staff Sgt. Joel Salgado

Support RAND
Make a tax-deductible charitable contribution at
www.rand.org/giving/contribute

www.rand.org

Preface

The ability to assess Department of Defense efforts to build partner capacity is in increasing demand. This research built on previous RAND work in this area and used detailed case studies, analyzed individually and collectively, to provide a foundation of evidence to help improve assessment of building partner capacity efforts, which should ultimately support future resource allocation and policymaking for building partner capacity and security cooperation more broadly.

The assessment framework should be of interest to policymakers and stakeholders in the broader security cooperation arena in the Office of the Secretary of Defense, the regional combatant commands (and the related service components), planners in the departments of Defense and State, and congressional staffs that deal with security assistance to partner nations. Readers may also be interested in

- Christopher Paul, Jennifer D. P. Moroney, Beth Grill, Colin P. Clarke, Lisa Saum-Manning, Heather Peterson, Brian Gordon, *What Works Best When Building Partner Capacity in Challenging Contexts?* Santa Monica, Calif: RAND Corporation RR-937-OSD.
- Christopher Paul, Colin P. Clarke, Beth Grill, Stephanie Young, Jennifer D. P. Moroney, Joe Hogler, and Christine Leah, *What Works Best When Building Partner Capacity and Under What Circumstances?* Santa Monica, Calif.: RAND Corporation, MG-1253/1-OSD, 2013.
- Christopher Paul, Michael Nixon, Heather Peterson, Beth Grill, and Jessica Yeats, *RAND Security Cooperation Prioritization and Propensity Matching Tool*, Santa Monica, Calif.: RAND Corporation, TL-112-OSD, 2013.
- Jennifer D. P. Moroney, David E. Thaler, and Joe Hogler, *Review of Security Cooperation Mechanisms Combatant Commands Utilize to Build Partner Capacity*, Santa Monica, Calif.: RAND Corporation, RR-413-OSD, 2013.

A controlled-access companion annex supports this report with case study details. That annex is available to those with a need to know and appropriate clearances.

This research was sponsored jointly by the Joint Staff J5, the Office of Cost Assessment and Program Evaluation in the Office of the Secretary of Defense, and the Office of the Under Secretary of Defense for Policy. The study was conducted within the

International Security and Defense Policy Center of the RAND National Defense Research Institute, a federally funded research and development center sponsored by the Office of the Secretary of Defense, the Joint Staff, the Unified Combatant Commands, the Navy, the Marine Corps, the defense agencies, and the defense Intelligence Community under contract W91WAW-12-C-0030.

For more information on the International Security and Defense Policy Center, see http://www.rand.org/nsrd/ndri/centers/isdp.html or contact the director (contact information is provided on the web page).

Contents

Figures and Tables

Figures

Tables

Summary

Security cooperation remains an important instrument of the U.S. government and the Department of Defense. One of the key challenges in this area for policymakers and combatant commands is gaining a more-complete understanding of the real value of activities geared toward building partner capacity (BPC). Assessments of prior and ongoing BPC activities have become increasingly important, given the current fiscal climate and budgetary limitations. Efforts that can be made to work more efficiently should be; efforts that are not working need to be recognized and redesigned, terminated, or replaced. Effective assessment provides a good analytic foundation from which to make process improvements or to focus accountability and resource allocation.

This report provides a framework for planning and conducting assessment of BPC efforts. It primarily supports planning and process improvement but can also contribute to assessment for accountability.

This BPC assessment framework should help a potential user answer one (or more) of three questions, depending on when in the BPC process the framework is employed:

- Prior to execution, **what could go wrong with the planned BPC effort?**
- During BPC execution or delivery, **is everything going according to plan? If not, why not, and what can be done about it?**
- After BPC execution or delivery, **were all objectives achieved? If not, why not, and what could be done about it in the future (either in this context or elsewhere)?**[1]

Methods and Approach

To develop an assessment framework for BPC, we drew on our familiarity with the literature on assessment and evaluation, and on experience with assessment of differ-

---

[1] The framework offered here is fundamentally about assessing performance, not assessing needs or determining requirements. This framework assumes that a prior process has concluded that BPC is the right approach to supporting U.S. national security objectives for and in the country in question.

ent activities.[2] A *theory of change* is a statement of how you believe the things you are planning to do will lead to the objectives you seek. Implicit in many examples of effective assessment and explicit in much of the work of scholars of evaluation research is the importance of a theory of change to effective evaluation. The theory of change for an activity, line of effort, or operation is the underlying logic for how planners think elements of the overall activity, line of effort, or operation will lead to desired results.

This report uses a logic model as the cornerstone of the BPC assessment framework. A logic model is one way to collect and express the elements of a theory of change. Logic models traditionally include inputs, outputs, and outcomes; some styles of logic model also report activities (connecting inputs and outputs) and results (long-term outcomes). In addition to specifying inputs, activities, outputs, outcomes, and results, logic modeling provides an opportunity to think about things that might go wrong. Which assumptions are the most vulnerable? Which of the inputs are most vulnerable to delays? Which of the activities might an adversary disrupt or are contingent on the weather? Such things can be listed as part of the logic model and can be placed next to (or between) the nodes they might disrupt.

We approached the identification and refinement of logic model elements and their connections in two ways: deductively and inductively. Deductive input began from the top down and was based on previous experience and research on BPC, existing guidance, the extensive literature on the subject, and common sense and logic. The deductive contribution was primarily abstract or generic, summarizing characteristics from numerous experiences. Inductive input came from the results of four deep-dive case studies and was much more concrete and specific. Each case study contributed a case-specific preliminary logic model; the synthesis of four case-specific logic models with the broader, deductive logic model led to the initial BPC training and equipping logic model. The model was further refined (and demonstrated as a useful assessment tool) through application to the specific cases.

The BPC Training and Equipping Logic Model

The resulting BPC training and equipping logic model is generic across all forms of BPC that emphasize training, equipping, or a combination of these (which is a considerable proportion of all BPC activities). The model (contained in a sizable Microsoft Excel spreadsheet associated with this report) lists the inputs, activities, outputs, and outcomes that logically accumulate to successful BPC, as well as the disrupters and workarounds. To organize the logic model and increase clarity for use and presenta-

---

2   Christopher Paul, Jessica M. Yeats, Colin P. Clarke, and Miriam Mathews, *Assessing and Evaluating Efforts to Inform, Influence, and Persuade: Desk Reference*, Santa Monica, Calif.: RAND Corporation, RR-809/1-OSD, 2015; Jan Osburg, Christopher Paul, Lisa Saum-Manning, Dan Madden, and Leslie Adrienne Payne, *Assessing Locally Focused Stability Operations*, RR-387-A, 2014.

tion, the model includes additional horizontal and vertical divisions. The horizontal divisions are temporal-sequential divisions, separating the BPC process into the pre-engagement phase, the engagement phase, and the postengagement phase. Outputs for earlier phases are often inputs to later phases, and this division makes that clearer and the overall logic easier to follow. The vertical division is a categorization of inputs, formed by grouping like inputs with like. Figure S.1 illustrates the overall organization of the logic model.

At the far right of Figure S.1 are the highest-level outcomes BPC seeks to attain through training and equipping. These are the culminating objectives against which BPC success should be measured. At a fairly high level of abstraction, the following are the desired outcomes of BPC training and equipping:

1. **Capacity has been built:** Capable units have been formed and equipped in accordance with objectives.

Figure S.1
Notional Organization of the BPC Training and Equipping Logic Model

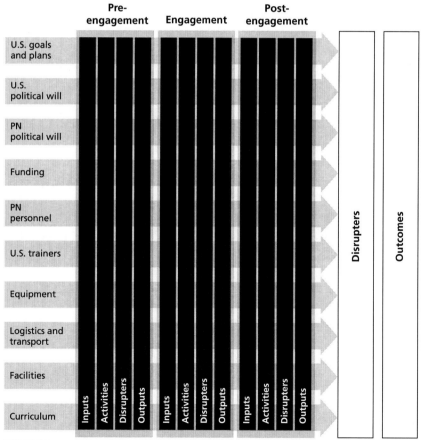

2. **That capacity is being sustained:** Maintenance and sustainment are occurring and training capability is being preserved (or has been institutionalized).
3. **A relationship with the partner nation (PN) has been created and is being preserved:** This makes further security cooperation possible.

Each sequential phase (preengagement, during engagement or delivery, postengagement) produces a set of core outputs that, cumulatively, lead to the core outcomes of the overall model. The *preengagement phase* involves planning, preparation, mobilizing funding, and marshaling political will and has the following core outputs:

1. identification of all needed inputs
2. preparation of all needed inputs
3. promotion of agreement and willingness (and resources) to provide all needed inputs.

The *engagement phase* is all about execution and delivery and has the following core outputs:

1. the delivery of effective training
2. the required number of trainees completing the program and achieving certification
3. adequate preservation of training facilities, materials, and other resources for next use, cycle, or rotation.

Item 2, the required number of trainees successfully completing training, is chief among the core outputs. Achieving it, however, depends on item 1, and being able to achieve it more than once depends on item 3.

The *postengagement phase* is about taking short-term training and equipping successes and transforming them into meaningful and enduring partner capacity. In this phase, sustainment is key: the maintenance and sustainment of units and their training; the maintenance and sustainment of equipment; and the maintenance and sustainment of relationships, both between elements of the PN and the United States and between relevant PN elements. The following are the core outputs of the postengagement phase:

1. use of trained (and equipped) personnel to form and man units, augment existing units, or train others (as specified in program's specific objectives)
2. continuing maintenance and sustainment of new forces and equipment, training facilities, and materials
3. continuing maintenance and sustainment of necessary relationships between and across U.S. and PN elements.

Figure S.2 summarizes these central elements of the BPC training and equipping logic model, listing the ten input categories, the three core outputs of each sequential phase, and the three core outcomes of the overall logic model.

Using the BPC Training and Equipping Logic Model as Part of an Assessment Framework

A logic model embodies the theory of change of a program or effort, the chain of logic that connects the resources provided and the activities conducted with production of the desired results and their consequences. Using a logic model, like the BPC training and equipping logic model, as part of an assessment framework allows the user to

Figure S.2
Input Categories, Phase Core Outputs, and Overall Outcomes for the BPC Training and Equipping Logic Model

	Pre-engagement outputs	Engagement outputs	Post-engagement outputs	Outcomes
U.S. goals and plans				
U.S. political will	1. Identification of all needed inputs	1. Delivery of effective training	1. Trained (and equipped) personnel are used to form and man units, augment existing units, or train others (as specified in objecitves)	1. Capacity is built: Capable units are formed and equipped in accordance with objectives
PN political will	2. Preparation of all needed inputs	2. Required number of trainees complete the program and achieve certification		
Funding	3. Agreement and willingness (and resources) to provide all need inputs	3. Training facilities, materials, and other resources adequately preserved for next use, cycle, or rotation	2. Continuing maintenance and sustainment of new forces and equipment, training facilities, and materials	2. Capacity is sustained: Maintenance and sustainment are occurring, and a training capability has been preserved (or institutional-ized)
PN personnel				
U.S. trainers				
Equipment			3. Continuing maintenance and sustainment of necessary relationships between and across U.S. and PN elements	3. The relationship with the PN continues: Relationships are created or preserved, making further security cooperation possible
Logistics and transport				
Facilities				
Curriculum				

RAND RR935-S.2

identify where the chain of logic might break or has broken. Breaks in the chain of logic could stem from some sort of execution failure (inputs not being provided, activities not being executed, or activities not being properly executed) or from some kind of disrupter or barrier that is preventing inputs from being transformed into outputs or is keeping outputs from realizing intended outcomes. Once a break or potential break in the chain of logic has been identified, steps can be taken to find a correction, repair, or workaround.

As noted previously, the logic model can be used prior to execution to support asking **what could go wrong with the planned BPC effort,** during execution to support asking **what is going wrong and what can be done about it,** and postexecution to ask **what did go wrong and how it could be done better next time.**

Depending in part on when the logic model is being applied and in part on what assessors already know, there are at least three ways to begin using the logic model for assessment:

- Left to right: Start with the input categories and trace connections and nodes across the logic model until problems (or possible problems) are found.
- Right to left: Begin on the far right of the logic model, with the highest-level outcomes. If any are deficient, work backward along the logic model paths that should lead to them until the break in the chain of logic is discovered, then seek to explain it.
- Radiating out from a specific node: If executor or manager input points out a specific problem or deficiency, find the logic model node that best captures that concern or issue, then explore adjacent nodes to see what the disruption might affect and how the disruption might be fixed or worked around.

Measurement in the BPC Training and Equipping Logic Model

In validations of the logic model on data from the four deep-dive case studies, we assessed logic model nodes qualitatively using categorical "stoplight" scores.[3] In most instances, these categorical scores proved to be perfectly adequate measures of the nodes of interest. That will usually be the case when using this logic model. For example, if delivery of equipment for training is "red" because the equipment was not delivered prior to the scheduled beginning of training, it is not particularly important to know exactly how many days the delivery was late. Knowing that gear was not present for training is sufficient to understand why training failed to meet equipment-related objectives. Understanding *why* the delivery was late is much more important than any

---

[3] Ultimately, we used slightly modified stoplights, including a fourth category, "orange," between "red" and "yellow" because "yellow" was given to too many nodes and contained both things that were not perfect but were not that bad and things that were pretty bad but not as disruptive as "red." Full details appear in the main text.

precise quantitative measurement of lateness. Reaching such an understanding may require further inquiry, but narrative inquiry, not something requiring further detailed measurement.

However, for certain logic model nodes, more-precise measurement provides additional benefits. For example, a training completion rate is a useful overall measure of training efficiency and requires only two measures to calculate: number of trainees beginning training and number of trainees satisfactorily completing training. Further, these numbers are both useful measures for accounting (and accountability) purposes in their own right. If the training completion rate is low, the specific reasons for trainees not completing training become interesting; circumstances will dictate whether the reasons need to be precisely quantified or whether a qualitative assessment will again be sufficient.

A thoughtful collection of informal and qualitative data and more-precise quantitative data should enable users to conduct useful assessments based on this framework. Users should not be concerned if application of the framework suggests measuring dozens of nodes because only a small fraction of the measurements are likely to need to be precise and to be at all demanding to collect.

Acknowledgments

We are indebted to our thoughtful and engaged sponsor points of contact: David Lowe and Louise Hoehl in the Office of Cost Assessment and Program Evaluation in the Office of the Secretary of Defense (OSD/CAPE), Maureen Bannon and Aaron Jay in the Office of the Under Secretary of Defense for Policy (OUSD[P]), and CAPT John Sniegowski and Sarah Braswell in the Joint Staff J5. Their guidance and support were instrumental in the development and dissemination of this report and its findings. We also owe debts of gratitude to several other DoD personnel who participated in earlier research in this area, attended interim briefings, commented on draft slides, or otherwise provided valuable feedback on the research: Timothy Bright, Thomas Johnson, and Melissa Kirkner of OSD/CAPE; James Miner of the Defense Security Cooperation Agency; and CAPT Connie Frizzell and CDR John Mann of the Joint Staff J5.

We thank several of our RAND colleagues who offered engaging discussion on this topic, foundational insights, or comments on draft materials: Seth Jones, Terrance Kelly, Thomas Szayna, Michael McNerney, and Jan Osburg. Joe Hogler, RAND adjunct staff, was instrumental in arranging and supporting interviews for one of our deep-dive case studies. RAND administrative assistant Maria Falvo, editor Phyllis Gilmore, and production editor Beth Bernstein contributed substantially to the form and fettle of the final product, as did the two scholars who reviewed this document as part of the RAND quality assurance process: Christopher Schnaubelt and James Schear.

Finally, we thank all the personnel in OSD, at the combatant commands, in the components, in the embassies and military groups, and elsewhere who took the time to share information and insights about BPC in the specific country cases. We refrain from thanking you all by name to keep the terms of our anonymous interviews, but you know who you are, and we appreciate your contributions.

Abbreviations

AAR	after-action review
AOR	areas of responsibility
BPC	building partner capacity
CCMD	combatant command
DoD	Department of Defense
IT	information technology
MILGP	military group
OPTEMPO	operational tempo
OSD/CAPE	Office of the Secretary of Defense for Cost Assessment and Program Evaluation
OUSD[P]	Office of the Under Secretary of Defense for Policy
PCS	permanent change of station
PN	partner nation
SME	subject-matter expert
SOF	special operations forces

CHAPTER ONE

Introduction

Security cooperation has long been an important instrument of the U.S. government and the Department of Defense (DoD) for advancing national security objectives vis-à-vis allies and partner countries, including building critical relationships, securing peacetime and contingency access, and building partner capacity (BPC). Assessment of these activities, however, has often been a shortcoming.

Assessment or evaluation is fundamentally a judgment of merit against criteria or standards.[1] But for what purpose? To what end do we make these judgments of merit? In other RAND research, we found that almost all types and classes of assessment align comfortably with one (or more) of three purposes: to improve planning, to improve effectiveness and efficiency, or to enforce accountability.[2] Within the bounds of these three purposes, assessments are primarily either about accountability to an external stakeholder (focused up and out) or designed to support planning or improvement internally (focused down and in).

This report provides a framework for planning and conducting assessment of BPC efforts. The primary focus of assessment conducted within this framework will be down and in; this framework primarily supports planning and process improvement. Improved planning for assessment also improves planning in general by identifying desired outputs and outcomes more clearly. The framework can also support assessment for accountability, but this is not its primary function.[3]

This BPC assessment framework should help a potential user answer one (or more) of three questions, depending on when in the BPC process the framework is employed:

---

[1] Peter H. Rossi, Mark W. Lipsey, and Howard E. Freeman, *Evaluation: A Systematic Approach*, Thousand Oaks, Calif.: Sage Publications, 2004.

[2] Christopher Paul, Jessica M. Yeats, Colin P. Clarke, and Miriam Mathews, *Assessing and Evaluating Efforts to Inform, Influence, and Persuade: Desk Reference*, Santa Monica, Calif.: RAND Corporation, RR-809/1-OSD, 2015.

[3] Note that the framework is focused on *performance* assessment, how a BPC effort will work, is working, or has worked. This framework is not useful for *needs* assessment (or requirements determination), the process of deciding that BPC is the appropriate way to pursue national security goals in a given context, or how much BPC is needed to meet or support theater security strategic objectives. Such decisions logically precede what is offered here and are beyond the scope of this effort but remain important.

- Prior to execution, this framework could help planners answer the question: **What could go wrong with the planned BPC effort?**
- During BPC execution or delivery, this framework could help managers answer the questions: **Is everything going according to plan? If not, why not, and what can be done about it?**
- After BPC execution or delivery, this framework could help managers answer the questions: **Were all objectives achieved? If not, why not, and what could be done about it in the future (either in this context or elsewhere)?**

Assessment contributes little to process improvement when everything is going well; as the old saying goes, "if it ain't broke, don't fix it." However, given the challenges inherent in BPC activities, everything rarely goes well. Some aspect of the process is less effective or efficient than planned, or something fails in a highly disruptive way. Good inward-focused assessment and assessment planning help answer one or more of the following questions and helps make needed improvements until everything (or enough things) goes right: What might go wrong? What is going wrong? What went wrong?

Study Background and Companion Reports

This report is one of two produced by a larger study completed in 2013 and 2014. The study combined and extended three existing strands of research sponsored by the Joint Staff J5, the Office of Cost Assessment and Program Evaluation in the Office of the Secretary of Defense (OSD), and the Office of the Under Secretary of Defense for Policy.[4] These three strands of research led to several important research questions, one of which is fundamentally about assessment: How can DoD best assess the effectiveness and efficiency of BPC efforts? This is the motivating question for this report.

Methods and Approach

The goal of this research was to develop a framework for planning and conducting assessment of BPC efforts with the overall goal of improving the effectiveness and efficiency of such efforts.

---

[4] See Christopher Paul, Colin P. Clarke, Beth Grill, Stephanie Young, Jennifer D. P. Moroney, Joe Hogler, and Christine Leah, *What Works Best When Building Partner Capacity and Under What Circumstances?* Santa Monica, Calif.: RAND Corporation, MG-1253/1-OSD, 2013; Christopher Paul, Michael Nixon, Heather Peterson, Beth Grill, and Jessica Yeats, *The RAND Security Cooperation Prioritization and Propensity Matching Tool,* Santa Monica, Calif.: RAND Corporation, TL-112-OSD, 2013; Jennifer D. P. Moroney, David E. Thaler, Joe Hogler, *Review of Security Cooperation Mechanisms Combatant Commands Utilize to Build Partner Capacity,* Santa Monica, Calif.: RAND Corporation, RR-413-OSD, 2013.

Implicit in many examples of effective assessment and explicit in much of the work by scholars of evaluation research is the importance of a *theory of change* to effective evaluation.[5] The theory of change for an activity, line of effort, or operation is the underlying logic for how planners think elements of the overall activity, line of effort, or operation will lead to desired results. Simply put, a theory of change is a statement of how you believe the things you are planning to do are going to lead to the objectives you seek. A theory of change can include logic, assumptions, beliefs, or doctrinal principles. The main benefit of articulating a theory of change in the assessment context is that it allows assumptions of any kind to be turned into *hypotheses*. These hypotheses can then be tested explicitly as part of the assessment process, with any failed hypotheses replaced in subsequent efforts until a validated, logical chain connects activities with objectives and objectives are met. This is exactly what is described in the *Commander's Handbook for Assessment Planning and Execution*: "Assumptions made in establishing cause and effect must be recorded explicitly and challenged periodically to ensure they are still valid."[6] A theory of change is useful for assessment purposes but is also useful for the *design* of an effort or program. Including a clear theory of change in the design of a BPC effort could help implementers

- make assumptions explicit about what change is expected and how and why that change is expected
- weed out unrealistic program ideas and refine and clarify new ideas
- uncover gaps in planned programming where steps in the proposed logic are mistaken or missing
- make sure everyone involved in the program has the same understanding of how it is supposed to work.[7]

Logic Model Basics

A logic model is one way to collect and express the elements of a theory of change: "The logic model is supposed to make the program's theory of change explicit. A theory of change describes how the activities, resources, and contextual factors work together to achieve the intended outcome."[8] We chose to use logic models as the cornerstone of the BPC assessment framework.

---

[5] Some of the discussion in this section is drawn directly from Christopher Paul, "Foundations for Assessment: The Hierarchy of Evaluation and the Importance of Articulating a Theory of Change," *Small Wars Journal*, Vol. 10, No. 3, 2014.

[6] Joint Chiefs of Staff, *Commander's Handbook for Assessment Planning and Execution*, Suffolk, Va.: J-7, Joint and Coalition Warfighting, Version 1.0, September 9, 2011, p. II-10.

[7] Eileen Babbitt, Diana Chigas, and Robert Wilkinson, *Theories and Indicators of Change: Concepts and Primers for Conflict Management and Mitigation*, Washington, D.C.: U.S. Agency for International Development, 2013.

[8] Donna M. Mertens and Amy T. Wilson, *Program Evaluation Theory and Practice: A Comprehensive Guide*, New York, N.Y.: The Guilford Press, 2012, p. 244.

Logic models traditionally include effort inputs, outputs, and outcomes. Some styles of logic model development also report activities and impacts. Figure 1.1 presents these elements in sequence.

Inputs, Activities, Outputs, Outcomes, and Impacts

The *inputs* to a program or effort are the resources required to conduct the program. These will, of course, include personnel and funding but can also include guidance, agreements, authorities, and plans (among other things). Inputs are often enumerated more precisely than the general categories listed in the previous sentence, perhaps indicating specific expertise required, numbers of personnel (or person hours or effort available), etc. An effort's *activities* are the verbs associated with the use of the inputs and are the undertakings of the program; these might include transportation and delivery of equipment or bringing together instructors, curriculum, and trainees within training facilities to deliver training. Activities involve the use of inputs to create outputs. In fact, some logic model templates omit activities, as activities just connect inputs to outputs and can often be inferred by imagining what has to be done with the inputs to generate the outputs.

Outputs are produced by conducting the activities with the inputs. Outputs include things that would be counted as part of traditional measures of performance and indicators that the activities have been executed as planned. These might include execution records, attendance records, and course completion rates. *Outcomes* (or effects) are "the state . . . that a program is expected to have changed."[9] This is the result of the overall process: The inputs resource the activities, and the activities produce the outputs. The outputs lead to the outcomes (or, as noted, outputs can be inputs to other parts of a process, leading to further outputs, and eventually to outcomes). The connection between outputs and outcomes is a critical juncture from a theory-of-change perspective because the mechanism that connects the outputs (training deliv-

Figure 1.1
Logic Model Template

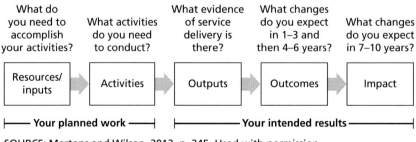

SOURCE: Mertens and Wilson, 2012, p. 245. Used with permission.
RAND RR935-1.1

---

[9]   Rossi, Lipsey, and Freeman, 2004, p. 204.

ered, trainees certified) to the outcomes (units formed and assigned) is a potentially vulnerable assumption. Outcomes are characteristics or behaviors of the recipients, not of the program or effort. The outputs are related to the program or effort and describe the products, services, or messages the program provides. Outcomes refer to the results (or lack of results) of the outputs produced, not just their delivery or receipt.[10]

The *impact* of a program or effort is the expected cumulative, long-term, or enduring contribution. There is no clear dividing line between immediate and short-term outcomes, medium-term outcomes, and long-term impacts. In fact, impact is beyond the scope of the BPC portion of the activities in many cases, being part of broader U.S. security cooperation or even foreign policy objectives.

Constraints, Barriers, Disrupters, and Unintended Consequences

In addition to specifying inputs, activities, outputs, outcomes, and impacts, logic modeling provides an opportunity to think about things that might go wrong. Which assumptions are the most vulnerable? Which of the inputs are most likely to be late? Which of the activities might an adversary disrupt or are contingent on the weather? These things can be listed as part of the logic model, and placed next to (or between) the nodes they might disrupt. For example, if local contractors might abscond with funds allocated for training facility maintenance or if training exercises are vulnerable to weather that can wash out roads and prevent participants from arriving at the training site, these things could be noted between the relevant input and activity. If partner nation (PN) posttraining personnel assignment policies can prevent the translation of an output (certified trainees) into a longer-term outcome (formed units), it could be noted between outputs and outcomes.

Barriers, or "disrupters," do not necessarily completely disrupt processes (although some do), but all will at least slow down or diminish the rate of success, the rate (or efficiency) of conversion of inputs into outputs, or outputs into outcomes. Perhaps they are best thought of as being like the coefficient of friction in physics. A severe enough disrupter has a coefficient of 1, wholly precluding progress past it (a barrier); a minor disrupter might have a coefficient of 0.2, causing just 20-percent inefficiency in the conversion of an input to an output. Depending on the context, 20-percent inefficiency may be an acceptable level of inefficiency.

Workarounds

If desired levels of results (either outputs or outcomes) are not being produced and if an identified disrupter is measured as being present, perhaps adjustments can be made. These adjustments might simply be to put more of an input or activity in place (realizing that a certain amount is being lost to "friction") or to identify some kind of workaround to minimize or remove the impact of the disrupter. If a logic model includes possible disrupters, it can also include possible workarounds.

---

[10] Rossi, Lipsey, and Freeman, 2004.

Logic Modeling for BPC

Ideally, every BPC program or effort would have its own explicit theory of change and its own well-developed logic model based on that theory. In practice, however, theories of change are often left implicit and are not articulated, and busy action officers often lack the time, training, and experience necessary to assemble a useful logic model. Fortunately, the logic underlying many BPC efforts is very similar. Our approach to developing an assessment framework for BPC began with the intention of developing one or more generic logic models to cover a range of BPC activities in a range of contexts. The specific range of activities was, at the outset, an open question. We were aware that BPC takes different forms and is used to pursue a range of different activities. We were also aware that different logic model elements can be described at different levels of abstraction (from specific to quite generic and anywhere in between) and that different types of activities or types of contexts might require different levels of abstraction for effective assessment. Just how many specific logic models would ultimately be required?

In previous work, we synthesized the wide range of goals that BPC is used to pursue into six BPC objective areas: five capacity-building objectives and a sixth objective that is not about capacity building but that is a foreign-policy objective pursued through BPC efforts (numbered "A" below to indicate its qualitative difference from objectives 1 through 5).[11] These are:

1. internal security, including counterinsurgency, counterterrorism, and forces for counternarcotics[12]
2. conventional forces for self-defense and regional security, including air and missile defense and coalition operations
3. specialty forces for external use, including counterterrorism, peacekeeping, peace enforcement, humanitarian assistance, reconstruction, other stability operations, counterpiracy, and counternarcotics
4. ministerial capacity, defense institution creation, and reform
5. border security, along with maritime security, counterpiracy, countertrafficking, and crop eradication
A. relationship building or maintenance, securing access.

We hoped to develop logic models covering as many of the five BPC objective areas as possible, recognizing that each area might require its own logic model or that

---

[11] Paul, Clarke, et al., 2013.

[12] This category is substantially overlapping with what some DoD audiences prefer to discuss as Foreign Internal Defense.

specific classes of activity within each BPC area might require their own specific logic models.[13]

Deductive and Inductive Contributions to Logic Model Development

To develop generic BPC assessment logic models, we sought to populate inputs, activities, outputs, outcomes, disrupters (between each of the other categories of elements), and possible workarounds or solutions for the disrupters. We approached the identification and refinement of logic model elements and their connections both deductively and inductively. First, we began to model deductively, from the top down, in an abstract way based on our experience and research on BPC, existing guidance, the extensive literature on the subject, and common sense and logic. This deductive effort produced the large frame for the logic models and most of the specific model elements. Second, we sought inductive input from case studies. We built provisional logic models for the BPC efforts conducted in four cases (case selection is described later in this chapter). These case-specific logic models captured specific inputs, outputs, and disrupters that were important in these particular cases. The synthesis of four case-specific logic models with the broader deductively based logic model led to our initial BPC training and equipping logic model. This model was further refined (and demonstrated as a useful assessment tool) through application to the specific cases.

We elected to allow the number of logic models required and their level of specificity to be an empirical question whose answer would be based on the demonstrated effectiveness of draft logic models in the empirical cases. Ultimately, we concluded that the vast majority of BPC activities could be captured in a single logic model, a logic model for BPC training and equipping. Most activities in BPC objective areas 1, 2, 3, and 5 can be assessed based on this logic model. However, activities in BPC objective area 4, ministerial capacity building, are fundamentally different. Less about training and equipping, ministerial capacity building is about engagement, education, mentoring, and advising. More, while the outputs and outcomes for training and equipping are sufficiently similar across objective categories and contexts to be generalized into a single model, the outputs needed in ministerial capacity building vary from case to case, depending on the specific strengths and weaknesses of the ministry in question.

---

[13] Note that the five BPC objective areas are constrained to capacity-building objectives—improving the capability and effectiveness of PN forces—and do not extend to broader national security objectives that such capacity building might serve. The sixth objective area deals with relationships or access, broader goals regarding what the PN might *do* with the capacity built. The implicit theory of change that supports our logic modeling efforts is constrained, then, to increasing capacity levels without theorizing about other changes that may be needed to meet national security objectives, such as changes in PN willingness to deploy their forces or in PN support for various U.S. policies or operations. This limitation (which the scope of this effort made necessary) allowed the assessment framework to be somewhat generic and to cover the capacity-building portion of a wide range of BPC efforts while excluding the connection between capacity building and broader national security objectives. See the discussion of nested logic models under "Nested Logic Models" in the next chapter.

We were able to complete a single comprehensive logic model for BPC training and equipping that covers (and will support assessment of) most of the activities of most BPC objective areas. The next chapter presents this model in detail. We recognize the need for an additional model or models to support ministerial capacity building but were unable to complete such a model with the time and resources available. This remains an important possible topic for future research.

Case Selection

Case selection for these analyses was bounded by a number of constraints and preferences. Many of these constraints were not particularly methodological but had to do with resource constraints and stakeholder equities. Other constraints were methodological but were relevant only to the other strand of research being supported using these same cases.[14] Case selection constraints were as follows:

- **There should be a total of between three and six cases.** Previous experience analyzing case studies for U.S. BPC efforts left us prepared for the fact that such cases are usually both complicated and poorly documented.[15] To be able to collect case data to the desired depth with the resources available, we had to limit the cases to a manageable target number.
- **All cases should represent instances of BPC in challenging contexts.** While not being of primary relevance to this inquiry, this constraint ensured identification of a wider range of disrupters than if the case contexts were less challenging.
- **Outcomes should vary.** This constraint was also not of primary relevance, but including less-successful cases ensured exposure to ways in which the logic of BPC could be threatened and supported identification of critical disrupters.
- **The cases should involve significant levels of U.S. BPC engagement.** In addition to wanting cases that included contextual challenges, we wanted to be able to examine efforts to conduct BPC while facing contextual challenges, which required some level of U.S. BPC engagement. Further, the presence of more effort would provide more data points, so we favored a significant level of BPC engagement.
- **The cases should have some history of U.S. BPC engagement.** Similarly, we sought cases in which U.S. BPC had been going on for some time, so that it would be possible (and meaningful) to consider its level of success. Countries that have only recently become the object of significant BPC efforts would have been less useful.

---

[14] See Christopher Paul, Jennifer D. P. Moroney, Beth Grill, Colin P. Clarke, Lisa Saum-Manning, Heather Peterson, Brian Gordon, *What Works Best When Building Partner Capacity in Challenging Contexts?* Santa Monica, Calif.: RAND Corporation, RR-937-OSD, forthcoming.

[15] See Paul, Clarke, et al., 2013.

- **The cases should represent multiple BPC objective areas.** We sought cases in which BPC efforts spanned more than one BPC objective area. A case with multiple objective areas would allow us to see whether challenging contexts affect different BPC areas differently. Further, the multiple BPC objective areas would allow us to develop and test assessment frameworks applicable across areas.
- **The cases should have BPC objective areas in common.** Just as having multiple BPC objective areas available has analytic benefits, having one or more BPC objective areas common to one or more cases would be useful for discerning whether observed differences were due to differences in contextual challenges, other differences in context, or differences in BPC due to the different objective areas.
- **In no case should "relationship building" be a primary BPC objective area.** As we have noted elsewhere,[16] conducting BPC primarily to build relationships or gain access has importance qualitative differences from conducting BPC primarily to build actual capacity. While relationship building is an important part of foreign policy and security cooperation more broadly, we preferred cases that focused primarily on capacity building for developing assessment methods and identifying effective practices within challenging contexts.
- **Multiple combatant command (CCMD) areas of responsibility (AORs) should be represented.** So that the final set of cases would be broadly representative of the kinds of context in which the United States conducts BPC and to include multiple CCMD stakeholders in the research process, we sought cases from multiple CCMD AORs.

To identify candidate cases that jointly met these criteria, we began with data already available to RAND. We considered 29 cases from RAND previous research to form a preliminary list.[17] DoD considers the specific cases discussed (both candidates throughout the selection process and those ultimately selected) to be sensitive, so we have not listed them anywhere in this report. We drew the examples throughout this report from cases familiar to us, including examples outside the 29 studied in previous research and the four studied in detail in support of this effort. Readers should *not* assume that cases mentioned by name are necessarily cases selected as part of this process and studied specifically for this project.

In addition to the 29 cases for which we already had substantial data, we drew on global data from other RAND research to identify countries with low propensity for BPC success.[18] Of the 29 cases with which we began, 13 did not have relationship building or access as a primary BPC objective **and** were in the bottom half of overall

---

[16] Paul, Clarke, et al., 2013.

[17] Paul, Clarke, et al., 2013.

[18] Paul, Nixon, et al., 2013.

propensity scores (a first-cut proxy for having challenging contextual features) and so qualified as initial candidates.[19]

We also prepared a list of all countries in the bottom half of overall BPC propensity scores. We reviewed this list jointly with sponsors to make sure we were considering other cases of potential interest (additional cases from underrepresented CCMDs or cases that had been prominent in recent discussions inside sponsor organizations and thus might serve other interests if studied). This review led to the addition of eight candidate cases to our existing list of 13.

We began preliminary data collection on this list of 21 initial candidates to ascertain which collection of cases best met the selection criteria. A quick review of the BPC funding history for all candidates quickly revealed that efforts in four of the candidates were too nascent to satisfy that criterion, for example. After compiling preliminary data and reviewing results, we identified (in concert with the sponsor) eight cases as serious candidates that appeared to meet all selection criteria.

We then collected additional data on each of these eight cases for a viability review prior to selecting the final cases. Four of the eight cases were confirmed as strong candidates (additional data collection validated their satisfaction of individual case criteria, and as a set, they adequately satisfied collective case criteria). With the sponsors' concurrence, we elected to move forward to intensive ("deep-dive") case study data collection and analyses for these four cases.

The four selected cases satisfy all the case-selection criteria. All were confirmed as cases of BPC in challenging contexts; the level of success of the BPC efforts varied, both within and between cases; all had significant histories of significant BPC engagement; each came from a different CCMD AOR; and they included three different BPC objective areas (four cases included BPC for border security or maritime forces; four cases included ministerial capacity building; and three cases included BPC for forces for internal security).

These four cases are not "statistically" representative (that is, they were not randomly selected from a specified population, and the probability that they might have been selected from such a population cannot be meaningfully quantified). However, they were chosen in accordance with a reasonable set of criteria and were intended to be broadly representative of a range of BPC activities and a range of contextual challenges that such activities might face. We used each case heuristically, to contribute to the development of a model rather than to test (or quantify) the effectiveness of specific variables. While confidence in the generalizability of findings based on these cases cannot be precisely quantified, the results make sense intuitively, correspond with the authors' collective experience with BPC, and are likely to hold across a wide range of similar efforts and contexts. Although we developed the assessment framework using BPC conducted in challenging contexts, the resulting framework is also applicable

---

[19] Paul, Nixon, et al., 2013.

in less-challenging contexts. The BPC logic model (described beginning in the next chapter) does contain elements that are specific to challenging contexts, but these can be safely ignored (or simply scored as not present or not applicable) in less-challenging contexts.

Throughout the remainder of the report, we use open-source examples to illustrate elements of the BPC training and equipping logic model. The examples we drew from include cases beyond the four selected ones, cases with which we are familiar that successfully illustrate a point. Mention of a specific country case elsewhere in the report should not lead the reader to assume that it is one of four selected core cases.

Outline of the Remainder of the Report

Chapter Two introduces the BPC training and equipping logic model and its organizing principals. Chapter Three describes the logic model elements in the preengagement phase; Chapter Four describes elements in the engagement phase; and Chapter Five describes both elements in the postengagement phase and highest level outcomes. Chapter Six offers practical advice for using the logic model in a number of different ways as part of a larger assessment framework. There are no conclusions and recommendations because our goal was only to produce an assessment framework. The sole recommendation, then, is to make use of the framework in support of BPC assessment and design, as outlined in Chapter Six, as appropriate.

CHAPTER TWO

The BPC Training and Equipping Logic Model

This chapter begins the presentation of the BPC training and equipping logic model that is foundational to the assessment framework developed as part of this research. The subsequent three chapters complete the presentation, with each chapter describing all the elements of one logic model phase (preengagement [pre-], during engagement [during], and postengagement [post-]). This chapter is expository, walking through the logic of BPC through training and equipping and breaking that logic down into inputs, activities, outputs, and outcomes; disrupters between these stages; and possible workarounds for disrupters.

Nested Logic Models

BPC is a subordinate element of security cooperation more broadly, which itself is a subordinate element of national security policy. BPC is and should be integrated into broader security cooperation and foreign policy activities; ideally, all these things should be assessed. However, we believe it is possible to assess BPC in a strictly programmatic sense, focusing on performance in relation to capacity building and not on BPC's (very important) connection to larger national security objectives.

From a logic modeling perspective, this implies several nested logic models. In this view, the largest logic model would be for national security, in which security cooperation would be one line of possible inputs and outputs available to contribute to foreign policy outcomes, and BPC would be one line of inputs and outputs subordinate to security cooperation. Each of these nested lines of effort could be a logic model in its own right. See Figure 2.1. In this nested logic model view, there is always more logic model potentially both to the "left" and to the "right" of the model at hand. To the left are all the things logically prior to the inputs. If inputs include plans, the decisional processes that led to a need for plans and the generation of the plans would come first. If inputs include personnel, the recruitment and training of these personnel would logically come first. To the right are larger processes and objectives, as well as longer-term, higher-level outcomes and impacts. So, in a sense, all of BPC can (accu-

Figure 2.1
The BPC Logic Model as a Subordinate Element of the Security Cooperation Model and, in Turn, of the National Security Model

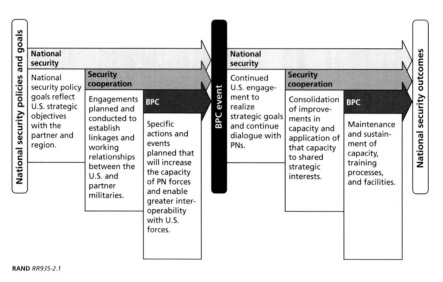

rately) be thought of as an input toward producing broader national security and foreign policy outputs.

Deciding where to bound a logic model (both on the right and left) is at least as much art as science. There is constant pressure to continue in both directions. To the left, details cry out to be added; to the right, there is a constant pull to make the connection all the way to broader strategic objectives and national security goals. We made conscious and intentional decisions about the bounds of this logic model. This is *only* a BPC logic model, with the model ending on the right with outcomes concerning capacity being built and sustained. While the model certainly points toward broader security cooperation and still broader foreign policy outcomes and impacts, it does not include them. This leaves the possibility that a framework using this logic model could declare a BPC event a success (all capacity building and sustainment outputs and outcomes haveing been achieved), while a foreign policy or strategic-level assessment might view the event as a failure, because built capacity was not used or was not used in ways that aligned with broader objectives. While those planning and executing BPC must keep larger strategic objectives in mind, assessment of success at BPC can and should be separate and different from assessment of broader foreign policy success.[1]

Another way in which logic models nest concerns the sequence of elements. During preliminary collection of elements for draft logic models for this project, we

---

[1] This view corresponds with the aphorism, "the operation was a success, but the patient died." In the operating room and in the security cooperation domain, this can happen. Strategic choices about where or where not to conduct BPC because of possible variations in whether successful BPC will contribute to broader foreign policy goals are very important. They are also, however, beyond the scope of this report.

routinely noted that outputs from one part of the process were inputs to another part of the process. For example, the outputs of the planning process were then inputs to execution. Although this made perfect sense, it provided a challenge for traditional logic modeling, in which inputs and outputs are listed separately. On further examination, we noticed that the sequences of outputs becoming inputs to later processes followed a clear time phase pattern. We experimented with breaking the model into three phases: a preengagement or delivery phase, an engagement or delivery phase, and a postengagement or delivery phase, with each phase having its own set of inputs, activities, outputs, and disrupters. This almost entirely resolved the problem. Under this scheme, outputs of the preengagement phase were often also inputs to the engagement phase, but were clearly indicated as outputs in the pre- portion of the model, and inputs in the during portion of the model. We preserved this exploratory separation, and the final model has submodels for each corresponding phase (pre-, during, and post-). Each submodel includes inputs, activities, outputs, disrupters, and workarounds for that phase of the process.

Target High-Level Outcomes in the BPC Training and Equipping Logic Model

The elements to the farthest right of the logic model are the high-level outcomes BPC sought to achieve through training and equipping. These are the culminating objectives against which BPC success should be measured. We begin on the far right (rather than on the left, at the "beginning") because a logic model should always have a clear destination. The importance of clear objectives to assessment is well documented elsewhere.[2] At a fairly high level of abstraction, the following are the desired outcomes of BPC through training and equipping (generic and able to be matched to the corresponding BPC area):

1. **Capacity is built:** Capable units have been formed and equipped in accordance with objectives.[3]
2. **Capacity is sustained:** Maintenance and sustainment are occurring, and training capability is being preserved (or has been institutionalized).
3. **The relationship with the PN continues:** Relationships are created or preserved, making further security cooperation possible.

---

[2]   Paul, Yeats, et al., 2015.

[3]   Exactly what levels of capability and capacity are desired needs to be detailed in a specific BPC plan; the logic model is generic regarding both.

All the outputs from the different sequential phases and the different input categories explicitly support the achievement of these three outcomes. They are listed at the top right of the full logic model spreadsheet but are then repeated as appropriate in the rightmost column of the logic model, at the end of each set of input category rows, to show which aspects of each input set support which outcomes.

Target Core Outputs of the Sequential Phases of the BPC Training and Equipping Logic Model

Each of the sequential phases (pre-, during-, and post-) produces a set of core outputs that, cumulatively, lead to the core outcomes of the overall model. Remember that the outputs of early phases are usually inputs to later phases.

The *preengagement phase* is a phase of planning, of preparation, of mobilizing funding and marshaling political will and has the following core outputs:

1. identification of all needed inputs
2. preparation of all needed inputs
3. agreement and willingness (and resources) to provide all needed inputs.

The *engagement phase* is all about execution and delivery and has the following core outputs:

1. delivery of effective training
2. required number of trainees complete the program and achieve certification
3. adequate preservation of training facilities, materials, and other resources for next use, cycle, or rotation.

Item 2, the required number of trainees successfully completing training, is chief among the core outputs. Achieving it, however, depends on item 1, and being able to achieve it more than once depends on item 3. For example, although an ample number of PN personnel may complete training, many often rotate out of the unit, taking what they have learned with them. Effective unit training cannot be achieved if that unit's key resource—its talent base—is in constant upheaval and thus institutional knowledge is not being adequately preserved.

The *postengagement phase* is about taking short-term training and equipping successes and transforming them into meaningful and enduring partner capacity. In this phase, sustainment is key: the maintenance and sustainment of units and their training; the maintenance and sustainment of equipment; and the maintenance and sustainment of relationships, both between elements of the PN and the United States and between relevant PN elements. The core outputs of the postengagement phase are:

1. trained (and equipped) personnel are used to form and man units, augment existing units, or train others (as specified in objectives)
2. continuing maintenance and sustainment of new forces and equipment, training facilities, and materials
3. continuing maintenance and sustainment of necessary relationships between and across U.S. and PN elements.

Figure 2.2 summarizes these central elements of the BPC training and equipping logic model, listing the ten input categories (listed in the next section), the three core outputs of each sequential phase, and the three core outcomes of the overall logic model.

Figure 2.2
Input Categories, Phase Core Outputs, and Overall Outcomes for the BPC Training and Equipping Logic Model

	Pre-engagement outputs	Engagement outputs	Post-engagement outputs	Outcomes
U.S. goals and plans				
U.S. political will	1. Identification of all needed inputs	1. Delivery of effective training	1. Trained (and equipped) personnel are used to form and man units, augment existing units, or train others (as specified in objecitves)	1. Capacity is built: Capable units are formed and equipped in accordance with objectives
PN political will	2. Preparation of all needed inputs	2. Required number of trainees complete the program and achieve certification	2. Continuing maintenance and sustainment of new forces and equipment, training facilities, and materials	2. Capacity is sustained: Maintenance and sustainment are occurring, and a training capability has been preserved (or institutional-ized)
Funding	3. Agreement and willingness (and resources) to provide all need inputs	3. Training facilities, materials, and other resources adequately preserved for next use, cycle, or rotation	3. Continuing maintenance and sustainment of necessary relationships between and across U.S. and PN elements	3. The relationship with the PN continues: Relationships are created or preserved, making further security cooperation possible
PN personnel				
U.S. trainers				
Equipment				
Logistics and transport				
Facilities				
Curriculum				

RAND RR935-2.2

Input Categories

In addition to the horizontal divisions in the logic model caused by arraying the sequential phases from left to right (and arraying inputs to outputs from left to right within phases), the model has vertical divisions.[4] These vertical divisions are categories that put like sequences of action next to each other. Since the primary organizing principle in creating these categories ended up corresponding very closely to grouping like inputs together, we label these categories "input categories." The model contains ten input categories.

U.S. Program Goals and Plans

This input category sets the stage for all the others and contains inputs related to planning and to connecting the proposed BPC activities to broader strategic goals and objectives. While in the terms of this logic model strategic outcomes are often "off to the right" of the model, many of the inputs in this category specifically point toward the higher-level intentions.

U.S. Political Will

To conduct an effective BPC program, the will to engage the PN, allocate resources, and execute a role in the effort must exist across the spectrum of U.S. policymaking. The stakeholders involved in this phase of the effort will likely vary by country and certainly by program size but may include Congress members and staff, National Security Council and other executive branch officials, or U.S. law enforcement agencies. At a minimum, the will for engagement must exist within the embassy and in-country team (including the military group [MILGP] if applicable) and the responsible CCMD.

This line of effort in the logic model addresses the need to gain, maintain, and continue program support among U.S. policymakers. Actions in this input category focus on outcome 3 (relationship). The intent is to generate support among U.S. officials, maintain it through efficient execution of the program, and ensure that support for future engagements is maintained.

PN Political Will

Just as political will among U.S. stakeholders is essential for planning and executing a successful BPC program, the willingness of PN officials to support the program is also essential. This political will may entail several more dimensions than does that of the United States. In this case, not only do senior- and ministerial-level officials need to be predisposed or convinced to support the BPC program, but the operational and mid-level defense officials also need to support it. A program may enjoy broad support in

---

[4]   Further note that, in practice, BPC efforts do not always progress linearly, with execution feedback loops that the logic model explicitly captures (or implies). An example would be that if a PN unit does not meet training objectives, program managers could loop back and retrain it.

Washington and in the PN's ministry, but without the concurrence of relevant operational, base, and unit commanders, the program is unlikely to be successful. As with U.S. political will, the desired end state of these actions is what has been identified as outcome 3 (relationship).

Funding

No BPC effort can be executed without timely and adequate funding. The source of that funding will vary from case to case, with the United States shouldering some or all of the burden in many scenarios. But whatever the ratio of funding the United States and the PN agree to provide, the total needs to be enough to ensure success or at least to get the program off the ground. For the purposes of this model, we assumed that neither side will proceed until both have agreed to an appropriate amount of funding and allocated it. Therefore, unlike the lines of effort for political will, we combined the contributions of the United States and its partner. The informative portions of the model in this line of effort are not necessarily the activities and outputs, which are largely intuitive, but the myriad disrupters that may complicate program implementation.

The overall outcome that the funding line of effort aims to produce is outcome 1 (capacity is built).

PN Personnel (Trainees)

The personnel the PN assigns to the BPC effort are a, if not the, key input to the process. It is these personnel who will ultimately facilitate the increase in capacity that the program seeks. The personnel assigned must be the right ones, be assigned on time, and be utilized following the program in a manner that will accomplish the program's goals. The allocation, assignment, and retention of PN personnel affect the building of capacity through overall outcome 1 (capacity is built) and outcome 2 (capacity is sustained).

U.S. Trainers

As essential as the right PN personnel are to a successful BPC effort, the trainers (who presumably come from the United States) are similarly essential. The right trainers must be assembled; briefed on the intent of the effort; transported; and provided with essential equipment, provisions, and safety measures throughout the process. This input category contributes primarily to overall outcome 1 (capacity is built) but can be important to institutionalization (outcome 2, capacity is sustained) and relationships (outcome 3) as well.

Equipment

The role of equipment will vary between training programs. It may be the entire focus of the training, an aid to facilitate training, or a parameter of PN operations that must be accounted for in developing the training program. The equipment used in a BPC effort may be what the PN has on hand, or the United States may give it or sell it to the PN. In any case, it is unlikely that a substantive BPC effort will be conducted in which equipment does not figure prominently. This line of effort is focused on providing the model's overall outcome 1 (capacity is built).

Logistics and Transport

Little capacity building can take place without a functioning logistics operation. This is even more true if the program is taking place within the PN and if U.S. officials must move people, equipment, and supplies to the location. PN forces may or may not be able to provide effective transport and logistics support. This is therefore a critical line of effort in determining the success of the BPC program. Outputs from the various stages of this effort support overall outcome 2 (capacity is sustained).

Facilities

Facilities include not only field training areas but also classroom space, office space for administration, living quarters, and force-protection requirements. For any BPC effort taking place in the PN, a significant amount of planning will revolve around the selection and suitability of facilities.

The activities in this line of effort support overall outcome 2 (capacity is sustained), and output 3 (relationship)

Curriculum, Program of Instruction, and Training Content

Although the previously discussed lines of effort are all essential to the success of the BPC program, it is the curriculum and training content that actually provides the potential for an increase in capability. Development and delivery of the curriculum are tasks that occur throughout each phase of the BPC program as the training program must be agreed on, delivered, and evaluated for improvements following the course. As such, this effort addresses all three of the model's overall outcomes.

BPC Training and Equipping Logic Model Overview

Thus the overall structure of the logic model runs the input categories as rows, and the sequential phases (pre-, during, post-) as columns, with each phase containing corresponding phase inputs, activities, disrupters, workarounds, and outputs. See Figure 2.3.

The next three chapters detail and describe the various elements of the BPC training and equipping logic model, giving open source examples where appropriate. Some of the examples are sanitized (omitting country and force details) to protect their sensitivity; other examples are drawn broadly from our experience with BPC, a pool of cases that is much broader than the four core cases that supported the development of this framework.

Figure 2.3
Notional Organization of the BPC Training and Equipping Logic Model

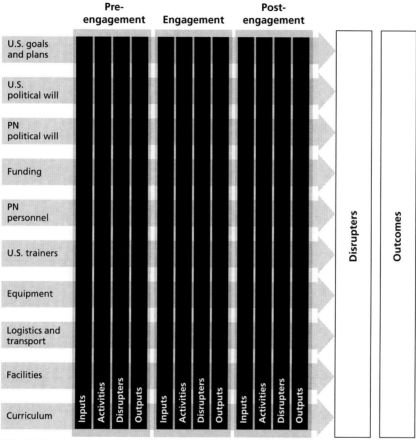

RAND *RR935-2.3*

CHAPTER THREE

Description of Logic Model Elements for the Preengagement Phase

Having presented the high-level objectives of the whole model (core outcomes) and of each sequential phase (phase core outputs), the discussion now turns to the logic of achieving these outputs and outcomes, detailing the inputs, activities, and subordinate outputs within each input category. We begin, in this chapter, with the preengagement phase. After presenting inputs, activities, and outputs, we also present things that can interfere with the progressive logic (the disrupters), and possible workarounds for those disrupters.

Many of the tables in this and subsequent chapters are sections of the larger logic model. The outputs are represented by the shaded blocks. Outputs that are sufficient but not ideal are in parentheses.

U.S. Program Goals and Plans: Preengagement

In the preengagement phase, this category contains seven inputs (Table 3.1). Two of these seek to match BPC plans with broader U.S. national security goals and CCMD objectives for the PN:

- identification of increased PN capabilities that would support U.S. goals
- identification of CCMD goals that this effort would support.

One input involves being able to explain and justify the need, the benefit, and the likely costs as risks:

- justification for direct U.S. involvement in country or for extending invitations for U.S. training.

Three inputs explicitly involve planning and coordination:

- a plan to increase PN capabilities that requires direct U.S. support
- assessment plans, including identification of observable measures of program accomplishment

Table 3.1
Logic Model: Preengagement Phase of the U.S. Goals and Plans Input Category

Specific Inputs	Activities	Disrupters (Activities–Outputs)	Workarounds (Activities–Outputs)	Subordinate Outputs—Ideal (Sufficient)	Category Phase Outputs Contribute to . . .
Identification of increased PN capabilities that would support U.S. goals		Disagreement on PN needs for training	Assess preengagement needs of current PN capabilities	Identification of issues that need to be resolved prior to training	
Plan to increase PN capabilities that requires direct U.S. support		Disagreement on resourcing			
Justification for direct U.S. involvement in country or for extending invitations for U.S. training	Coordinate plans between responsible U.S. government agencies and in-country team (embassy, MILGP, etc.)	Disagreement on methodology	Resolve at lowest organizational level possible	Coordinated plan and performance measures that all U.S. stakeholders agree with	
Identification of CCMD goals that are supported by this effort					
Assessment plans, including identification of observable measures of program accomplishment		Disagreement on program longevity			Phase core output 1, identification of all needed inputs
Coordination and deconfliction with other security assistance providers (interagency, international)	Identify points of contact, coordinators, and responsible U.S. units	Lack of continuity (personnel rotations, etc.)	Assign only U.S. personnel who will be available throughout program or for a required amount of time	Identification of supporting U.S. personnel and units	
			Engage appropriate attaché or other U.S. official who can engage with PN over the long term		
Understanding of PN political and military structure	Embassy and other in-country staff assess potential engagement points for U.S. officials	Lack of understanding of PN structures and personnel	Engage PN officials within the United States (or at the United Nations) to determine receptiveness to BPC and get recommendations for appropriate counterparts	Informed decisions about departments and levels with which to engage	

- coordination and deconfliction with other security assistance providers (interagency and international).

The final input is a prerequisite to effective BPC planning: understanding the PN political and military structure. Three principal activities involve transforming these prerequisite inputs into the subordinate outputs in this phase:

- coordinating plans between responsible U.S. government agencies and in-country team (embassy, MILGP, etc.)

- identifying points of contact, coordinators, and responsible U.S. units
- embassy and other in-country staff assessing potential engagement points for U.S. officials.

If the various stakeholders provide the inputs and conduct the activities, this input category should produce four subordinate outputs in this phase:

- identification of issues that need to be resolved prior to training
- agreement of all U.S. stakeholders on a coordinated plan and performance measures
- identification of supporting U.S. personnel and units
- making of informed choices about PN departments and levels with which to engage.

All these subordinate outputs contribute to phase core output 1 (identification of all needed inputs).

So, for example, improving the counterterrorism capabilities of PNs in vulnerable regions like the Middle East and South Asia would support overarching U.S. goals of combating violent extremist organizations like Al Qaeda and other groups of its ilk. To do so, U.S. planners must identify issues that need to be resolved prior to training, such as gaining PN support and acquiring congressional funding for U.S. military engagement. Many BPC efforts will be nested within a larger whole-of-government approach to security cooperation, so any specific BPC activities will need to be incorporated into the broader approach and ideally worked through a coordinating body that includes all key players. In one case we examined, this type of consultation process helped identify (sometimes competing) goals and facilitated discussions to help these U.S. entities communicate and sometimes act together to develop measures of performance to assess progress.[1] Gaining a more-comprehensive understanding of what type of assistance is needed and what other organizations are involved in the broader effort also helped DoD planners identify which U.S. personnel and units are best suited for the mission and allowed planners to make informed decisions regarding which PN entities they should focus their efforts on.

Disrupters (and Workarounds)

The logic model explicitly identifies six possible disrupters that can hinder the process at this phase and in this input category. Table 3.2 lists these disrupters and possible work-

---

[1]   The United States will also integrate the efforts of the host nations, nongovernmental organizations, and international organizations. For example, the Organization of American States is using funding provided under the Central American Regional Security Initiative to dispose of large quantities of seized drug precursor chemicals in Guatemala. Moreover, most projects implemented under the initiative include letters of agreement signed at the ministerial level.

arounds. This is neither an exhaustive list of the disrupters nor of the workarounds; other difficulties are possible, and alternative solutions may prove more effective in different contexts.

As an example of a disrupter, a lack of understanding of PN structures and an undiscovered disagreement on methodology became significant barriers to BPC success in one case we considered. In this case, the intended training model followed the train-the-trainer concept, in which U.S. trainers would train a cadre of PN trainers, who would then return to their units and pass on the training. However, this did not work as well as intended because the PN made no effort to place the trained trainers where they would be able to pass on their knowledge. Trained trainers rotated to other postings sooner than expected, often to postings without opportunities to train (staff or administrative roles) or to units that did not need the training in question.

U.S. Political Will: Preengagement

The preengagement phase of U.S. political will is the foundation of developing and planning the BPC engagement (Table 3.3). Two specific inputs exist in this phase. First, there must be a *desire to effect a change within the PN* that a BPC program could bring about. The broader U.S. policy goals for that country or the region must be served by a targeted increase in capacity within the PN's defense structure. The realization of U.S. goals must be clearly linked to the increase in PN capacity that the BPC program is intended to bring about. This cannot be taken for granted. For example, since establishment of limited Palestinian autonomy in the mid-1990s, the United States has given more than $5 billion U.S. dollars to the Palestinian Authority as part of the 2003 Roadmap for Peace process. This includes more than $392 million in assistance to the

Table 3.2
Disrupters and Workarounds: Preengagement Phase of the U.S. Program Goals and Plans Input Category

Disrupters	Workarounds
Disagreement on PN needs for training	Assess preengagement needs of current PN capabilities
Disagreement on resourcing	Resolve at lowest organizational level possible
Disagreement on methodology	Resolve at lowest organizational level possible
Disagreement on program longevity	Resolve at lowest organizational level possible
Lack of continuity (personnel rotations, etc.)	Assign only U.S. personnel who will be available throughout program or for a required amount of time
	Engage appropriate attaché or other U.S. official who can engage with PN over the long term
Lack of understanding of PN structures and personnel	Engage PN officials within the United States (or at the United Nations) to determine receptiveness to BPC and get recommendations for appropriate counterparts

Table 3.3
Logic Model: Preengagement Phase of the U.S. Political Will Category

Specific Inputs	Activities	Disrupters (Activities–Outputs)	Workarounds (Activities–Outputs)	Subordinate Outputs—Ideal (Sufficient)	Category Phase Outputs Contribute to . . .
Desire to effect change in PN	Brief program and goals to appropriate principals	Resistance at congressional, OSD, and/or CCMD levels	Ensure program design complies with statutory constraints, such as the Leahy Amendment	Authorizations and approvals to execute mission	Phase core output 2, preparation of all needed inputs
Determination of U.S. level of effort required for success		Resistance from in-country staff (embassy or MILGP)	—	Embassy and CCMD support for BPC efforts	Phase core output 3, agreement and willingness (and resources) to provide all needed inputs

Palestinian National Security Forces as of 2010.[2] Yet this support may contradict the U.S. policy of pursuing a two-state solution in two ways. First, U.S. support threatens to delegitimize the Palestinian National Security Forces by making them appear to be "Israel's cops" to residents of the territories.[3] Second, the fragmented nature of Palestinian governance risks the possibility of a power-sharing deal, with Hamas placing U.S.-funded and -trained security forces under the direction of a terrorist group. Indeed, such an agreement was brokered between Fatah and Hamas in April 2014, although the extent to which it would be implemented and the implications of the agreement were not clear as of this writing.

Second, a *determination of the required level of U.S. effort* must be made. As later facets of the logic model will address, the effort required for this increase in PN capacity may involve a combination of short-, medium-, and long-term activities. Multiple training iterations may need to be conducted. Maintenance and sustainment of equipment may need to remain a U.S. activity for some time.

The activity involved with this phase of U.S. political will is straightforward. The appropriate U.S. *principals must be briefed on the program and goals*, the desired PN change, and the level of commitment that change is expected to require. As previously stated, these principals may include congressional personnel for approval or appropriations, embassy staff for approval, and CCMD officials for resource allocation. The sufficient (and ideal) outputs for this activity are the *approvals to execute the mission* and *embassy support for BPC efforts*. These outputs contribute to phase core outputs 2 (preparation of all needed inputs) and 3 (agreement and willingness to provide all needed inputs).

---

[2]   U.S. Government Accountability Office, *Palestinian Authority: U.S. Assistance Is Training and Equipping Security Forces, but the Program Needs to Measure Progress and Faces Logistical Constraints*, Washington, D.C., GAO-10-505, May 2010.

[3]   Jim Zanotti, "U.S. Security Assistance to the Palestinian Authority," Washington, D.C.: Congressional Research Service, January 2010, p. 35.

Disrupters (and Workarounds)

The disrupter for this category in this phase is *resistance among any of the U.S. stakeholders*. Resistance among congressional, OSD, or CCMD officials will likely make it impossible to conduct any part of the BPC effort until all issues are resolved. For example, in more than one case examined, countries or specific military units within countries that failed to live up to international human rights standards were prohibited from receiving congressionally appropriated BPC funding. Reservations that U.S. principals have will need to be addressed before the program can move forward. Thus, one potential workaround to resistance from U.S. stakeholders is to ensure that the proposed program complies with all relevant statutes, such as the Leahy Amendment in the case of human rights standards.

Partner Nation Political Will: Preengagement

The preengagement phase consists of two specific inputs (Table 3.4). The first, very similar to that of the U.S. political will preengagement section, is a *willingness to affect a specific type of change within the PN's forces*. That change must be attainable through the BPC program and should be aligned as closely as possible to the U.S. conception of what capacities will be developed. A difference in the desired change between U.S. and partner personnel may cause issues to arise in the future.

The second specific input in this phase is *support on the part of partner officials for U.S. engagement and assistance*. In many countries or in certain situations, this type of engagement with the United States may involve either domestic or foreign political complications for the partner. While the support need not necessarily be public (many BPC activities could take place clandestinely or at least out of public view), PN officials would need to be comfortable with the prospect of accepting U.S. assistance to improve their own capabilities. For example, even for a long-standing partner, such as India, working with the United States can expose the incumbent government to criticism from opposition parties that wish to capitalize on Delhi's reputation as a proud and independent rising power.[4]

The activity for this phase consists only of *briefing the PN officials on the specifics of the planned BPC effort and discussing any modifications they may desire*. The subordinate outputs for this phase amount to a set of agreements between U.S. and PN officials on the goals and methods of the program. The first subordinate output is that the program briefed to the PN *satisfies both its requirements and those of the United States*. The second output is critical to a successful program—*the establishment of communications channels between U.S. and partner officials to address any issues that arise during the program*. This entails overall program acceptance, designating points of contact, and establish-

---

[4]   Manu Pubby, "Indo-US Exercise: Antony Wary of Political Fallout," *Indian Express*, September 6, 2011.

Table 3.4
Logic Model: Preengagement Phase of the PN Political Will Category

Specific Inputs	Activities	Disrupters (Activities–Outputs)	Workarounds (Activities–Outputs)	Subordinate Outputs—Ideal (Sufficient)	Category Phase Outputs Contribute to . . .
Desire to establish or increase capability within PN forces	Brief program goals to appropriate PN officials	PN supports BPC efforts but does not prioritize the mission BPC is intended to enhance	Plan dual-purpose BPC activities that satisfy both governments	A program plan that satisfies requirements of both U.S. and PN	Phase core output 1, identification of all needed inputs
		Disagreement exists between what PN wants and what United States thinks the PN needs	Enlist senior U.S. officials to argue for U.S. position; make changes if necessary		
PN leadership support of U.S. involvement in country		PN government and ministerial support are not communicated to or not shared by frontline units and personnel	Ensure PN leadership addresses PN personnel directly in support of BPC program	Program acceptance from PN officials and establishment of communication channels for issues during program (PN permission to tentatively move forward with the program or PN points of contact for continued coordination)	Phase core output 3, agreement and willingness (and resources) to provide all needed inputs
		PN is resistant because of concerns that U.S. training will unbalance internal power dynamics	Restructure training plan to address PN cultural and organizational concerns		
		PN support is lacking because of an honest misunderstanding or translation issue	Use embassy personnel with established relationships to communicate U.S. intentions		
		PN does not agree to focus on sustainment and maintenance	Specify that U.S. effort will not be expended without a viable sustainment plan following the program		
		Types or age of PN equipment present limitations	Restrict the scope of training effort to ensure that PN capable of meeting all requirements	(U.S. and PN agreement on an achievable set of training events)	Phase core output 3, agreement and willingness (and resources) to provide all needed inputs
		Disagreement exists over measures of student competence	U.S. and PN officials jointly establish standards and testing guidelines	Approval of formal standards for certification of students (U.S. and PN agreement on measurable improvements in trainee proficiencies)	

ing a schedule of communication among various individuals involved with the process. The third subordinate output is that *an attainable set of program events and standards for completion* must be agreed on to consider PN political will to be supportive of the BPC effort.

The outputs for the PN's political will differ slightly from those of the U.S. line of effort. Both aim to bring about phase core output 3 (agreement or willingness to provide all needed inputs for the program). Regardless of how much of the total funding or resources the United States contributes, assistance and support will almost certainly be needed to move equipment, disburse funds, or conduct other support activities that only the PN will be able to provide. In the case of PN political will, phase core output 1 (identification of all needed inputs) is also applicable. Without the support of the PN establishment, it is unlikely the United States will have sufficient visibility to determine the "who, when, and how" of the BPC program.

Disrupters (and Workarounds)

Obtaining approval from PN officials may be a delicate and complicated process. Several disrupters were identified in the preengagement phase for this effort (Table 3.5). Most of these disrupters relate to a mismatch between U.S. and PN goals or the means of pursuing them. In Colombia, early U.S. BPC efforts struggled because the U.S. goal was counternarcotics, while the Colombian goal was counterinsurgency. However, after September 11, 2001, both countries broadened their interests (with the United States having more interest in counterterrorism and the Colombians being more willing to be concerned about drug trafficking), and much greater levels of success were achieved.[5] In another one of the contemporary cases, misaligned security objectives were brought in line by building dual-use units that could achieve both U.S objectives (counterdrug operations) and PN priorities (population security, where needed).

Other disrupters relate to internal PN dynamics. The first of these is the possibility that *support from senior officials does not translate to support from operational or "frontline" personnel.* This disrupter deserves special consideration from U.S. planners because such an atmosphere may not be easy to detect before the BPC program starts. If there are concerns about the possibility of this situation, U.S. planners should attempt to arrange early and frequent visits and events involving senior PN officials

Table 3.5
Disrupters and Workarounds: Preengagement Phase of the PN Political Will Input Category

Disrupters	Workarounds
PN supports BPC efforts but does not prioritize the mission BPC is intended to enhance	Plan dual-purpose BPC activities that satisfy both governments
Disagreement exists between what PN wants and what United States thinks the PN needs	Enlist senior U.S. officials to argue for U.S. position; make changes if necessary
PN government and ministerial support are not communicated to or not shared by frontline units and personnel	Ensure PN leadership addresses PN personnel directly in support of BPC program
PN is resistant because of concerns that U.S. training will unbalance internal power dynamics	Restructure the training plan to address PN cultural and organizational concerns
PN support is lacking because of an honest misunderstanding or translation issue	Use embassy personnel with established relationships to communicate U.S. intentions
PN does not agree to focus on sustainment and maintenance	Specify that U.S. effort will not be expended without a viable sustainment plan following the program
Types or age of PN equipment present limitations	Restrict the scope of the training effort to ensure that PN is capable of meeting all requirements
Disagreement exists over measures of student competence	U.S. and PN officials jointly establish standards and testing guidelines

---

[5]   Peter DeShazo, Tanya Primiani, and Philip McLean, "Back from the Brink: Evaluating Progress in Colombia, 1999–2007," Washington, D.C.: Center for Strategic and International Studies, November 2007.

with a goal of communicating the ministry's support of the program to more-junior personnel. The second potential disrupter a reluctance of PN officials to participate out of concern that the training the United States provides will alter their internal power dynamics. There is no easy workaround for this disrupter because it comes from the PN's organizational culture. U.S. officials should recognize the issue and modify the program to the greatest extent possible to satisfy these concerns.

Funding: Preengagement

The specific inputs for the preengagement phase of funding are outputs from the same phases of U.S. and PN political will—*authorizations and approvals being in place to execute the mission and PN acceptance of the program* (Table 3.6). It is assumed that no funds can be allocated to the effort without buy-in from the policymakers of both countries. The activity for this phase is to *allocate the funds necessary to resource personnel, logistics, and training development.* The subordinate outputs are the United States and PN each providing the necessary funds to cover the their own responsibilities.

Funding activities in the preengagement phase addresses two outputs: phase core outputs 2 (preparation of all needed inputs) and 3 (agreement and willingness to resource all needed inputs).

Disrupters (and Workarounds)

Several disrupters were identified that may prevent achievement of the subordinate and core outputs (Table 3.7). These disrupters focus on the inability to provide the needed funding through bureaucratic delays, corruption, or allocation to only one specific set of units or missions.

Table 3.6
Logic Model: Preengagement Phase of the Funding Category

Specific Inputs	Activities	Disrupters (Activities–Outputs)	Workarounds (Activities–Outputs)	Subordinate Outputs—Ideal (Sufficient)	Category Phase Outputs Contribute to . . .
Authorizations and approvals in place to execute mission	Allocate funds to resource personnel, logistics, and training development	Funding or obligation of funds is delayed	Delay beginning of program	Necessary funds to cover U.S. responsibilities in program	Phase core output 2, preparation of all needed inputs
		It is difficult to disburse funds in country	Consider obligating funds to embassy		
		Funding is limited to units or activities in one particular sector (such as a specific border) that is not practical for PN	Delay beginning of program until funding can be opened to all necessary activities		
Program acceptance from PN officials and establishment of communication channels for issues during program	Allocate funds to resource personnel, logistics, and training development	Corruption diverts funding or other resources	U.S. oversees the resourcing system to the extent PN officials permit	Necessary funds to cover PN responsibilities in program	Phase core output 3, agreement and willingness (and resources) to provide all needed inputs
		Funding or obligation of funds is delayed	Delay beginning of program or resource from U.S. funds		

Table 3.7
Disrupters and Workarounds: Preengagement Phase of the Funding Input Category

Disrupters	Workarounds
Funding or obligation of funds is delayed	Delay beginning of program
It is difficult to disburse funds in country	Consider obligating funds to embassy
Funding is limited to units or activities in one particular sector (such as a specific border) that is not practical for PN	Delay beginning of program until funding can be opened to all necessary activities
Corruption diverts funding or other resources	U.S. oversees the resourcing system to the extent PN officials permit
Funding or obligation of funds is delayed	Delay beginning of program or resource from U.S. funds

One of the most common sources of friction in challenging contexts is corruption within PN bureaucracies. Equipment is sold on black markets instead of reaching its intended destination; customs agents seize portions of shipments in the name of unofficial "taxes"; and military leaders divert resources for personal gain. Corruption rarely causes the loss of all equipment or resources but does dramatically decrease the efficiency and throughput of inputs. For example, in Peru, the arrest of a notorious drug trafficker nicknamed "El Vaticano" and his relationship with Peru's head of intelligence, Vlad Montesinos, proved how disastrous corruption was for attempts to build PN counternarcotic capability in Peru.[6]

Partner Nation Personnel: Preengagement

The preengagement phase of the PN personnel line of effort focused on assignment and transportation of assigned personnel (Table 3.8). The specific input for this phase is an output from the PN political will effort—*PN personnel support for the BPC program*. It is assumed that, without support for the program from these officials, PN personnel assignment will be inappropriate, late, or insufficient.

The first activity in this phase is the *identification of PN personnel according to the program plan*. These are the personnel with the appropriate specialties, rank, and experience to build capacity in the manner intended. Second, either the PN or the United States acting through the partner must fund the *relocation of the identified personnel to the training facility*. Third, the *pay and subsistence of the assigned personnel must be funded*, again, either directly by the PN, directly by the United States or by the latter through the former. This is not a major point for more advanced militaries, but in one in which pay is still given out in cash, this activity can be logistically difficult. Finally, *PN authorities must be proactive in resourcing personnel* so that the program can start on time.

---

[6] Vanda Felbab-Brown, *Shooting Up: Counterinsurgency and the War on Drugs*, Washington D.C.: Brookings Institution Press, 2009, p. 59.

Table 3.8
Logic Model: Preengagement Phase of the PN Personnel Category

Specific Inputs	Activities	Disrupters (Activities–Outputs)	Workarounds (Activities–Outputs)	Subordinate Outputs—Ideal (Sufficient)	Category Phase Outputs Contribute to . . .
BPC enjoys the support of PN officials	Identify appropriate PN personnel according to plan	PN does not provide sufficient personnel	Suspend activity and reengage appropriate decisionmakers	(Assignment of sufficient PN personnel with appropriate qualifications as trainees)	Phase core output 2, preparation of all needed inputs
		Number of trainees assigned does not account for expected attrition rate			
		Culture clashes within PN forces, such as interservice or interdepartmental rivalries	Focus training on issues specific to civilian-military culture		
		Bureaucratic hurdles to vetting exist	Engage U.S. in-country team early to screen through International Vetting and Security Tracking		
		Insufficient personnel clear the vetting process	Train personnel immediately after basic training		
			Request that PN establish a new unit that is not engaged in disqualifying activities		
		Insufficient language-fluent PN personnel are available	Contract translators with appropriate backgrounds		
			Initiate language training in country (for example, with Defense Language Institute support)		
		Trainees lack the prerequisite basic familiarity with equipment or assigned tasks	Engage appropriate PN counterparts to reassign personnel		
			Modify training plan to include introductory section on basic skills, if practical		
	Fund relocation of trainees to facility	PN does not fund transfer of personnel	Use U.S. assets to relocate PN trainees		
	Fund trainee pay and subsistence	Corruption prevents trainees from receiving full pay; unequal pay compared with other services creates jealousy and resistance	Reform the payment process and/or equalize the pay structure		
	PN authorities resource trainees proactively	PN slow-rolls process or assigns inferior personnel to program	Suspend the activity and reengage appropriate decisionmakers		

The subordinate output for this phase is to assign a *sufficient number of PN personnel, with appropriate qualifications.* This supports the phase core output 2 (preparation of all needed inputs).

Disrupters (and Workarounds)

Numerous disrupters and workarounds for the assignment of PN personnel were identified in the model (Table 3.9). Most involve the PN's inability or lack of willingness to resource the appropriate personnel. However, two disrupters pertain to the vetting

Table 3.9
Disrupters and Workarounds: Preengagement Phase of the Partner Nation Personnel Input Category

Disrupters	Workarounds
PN does not provide sufficient personnel	Suspend activity and reengage appropriate decisionmakers
Number of trainees assigned does not account for expected attrition rate	Suspend activity and reengage appropriate decisionmakers
Culture clashes within PN forces, such as interservice or interdepartmental rivalries	Focus training on issues specific to civilian-military culture
Bureaucratic hurdles to vetting exist	Engage U.S. in-country team early to screen through International Vetting and Security Tracking
Insufficient personnel clear the vetting process	Train personnel immediately after basic training
	Request that PN establish a new unit that is not engaged in disqualifying activities
Insufficient language-fluent PN personnel are available	Contract translators with appropriate backgrounds
	Initiate language training in country (for example, with Defense Language Institute support)
Trainees lack the prerequisite basic familiarity with equipment or assigned tasks	Engage appropriate PN counterparts to reassign personnel
	Modify training plan to include introductory section on basic skills, if practical
PN does not fund transfer of personnel	Use U.S. assets to relocate PN trainees
Corruption prevents trainees from receiving full pay; unequal pay compared with other services creates jealousy and resistance	Reform the payment process and/or equalize the pay structure
PN slow-rolls process or assigns inferior personnel to program	Suspend the activity and reengage appropriate decisionmakers

of PN personnel by U.S. officials, both of which could lead to an inability to conduct an effective BPC effort.

Past human rights violations significantly restrict the number of personnel who can receive U.S. training. There is sometimes a significant and disappointing lag between improvements in human rights behavior and relaxation of attendant restrictions. In one case with enduring legacy human rights-based constraints, DoD worked only with vetted personnel assigned to select elite units. Unfortunately, this amounted to less than 3 percent of the entire PN security force. The partner in this case had more than 1,000 miles of coastline and multiple porous borders to patrol; hence, even the best equipped and best prepared of vetted personnel could achieve only a limited effect.

U.S. Trainers: Preengagement

There are two specific inputs for the U.S. trainers line of effort (Table 3.10). The first is the *coordinated plan agreed to by U.S. stakeholders* that was an output of the U.S. goals and plans category. It is this plan that informs how the team of trainers should be constituted. Second, a *sufficient number of personnel available to serve as trainers* is an input. If these are military personnel, they need to be taken off their current duties. If civilian, they must be hired and contracted to facilitate the program.

Table 3.10
Logic Model: Preengagement Phase of the U.S. Trainers Category

Specific Inputs	Activities	Disrupters (Activities–Outputs)	Workarounds (Activities–Outputs)	Subordinate Outputs—Ideal (Sufficient)	Category Phase Outputs Contribute to . . .
Agreement of U.S. stakeholders on a coordinated plan and performance measures	Assemble, train, and deploy a cadre with the ability to execute the training program according to plan	Trainers lack sufficient subject-matter or training expertise	Engage different contract trainers or another U.S. unit with more appropriate experience	(Trainers who are knowledgeable on subject matter and able to communicate material effectively to trainees)	Phase core output 2, preparation of all needed inputs
			Conduct preengagement training for trainers to acquire expertise		
		Trainers are insufficiently familiar with PN languages and customs	Contract interpreters with necessary technical expertise		
			Select trainers with previous experience in country or in countries with similar cultures		
			Conduct cultural familiarization training for U.S. personnel prior to engagement		
Sufficient personnel to serve as trainers		Trainers are unfamiliar with the goals and intent of the training	Conduct a preengagement orientation for trainers on the training plan and expectations		

These inputs lead to the only activity for this phase—*assembling, training, and deploying a cadre with the ability to execute the training program according to plan*. The subordinate output from this activity is *trainers who are knowledgeable on the subject matter and are able to communicate material effectively to trainees*. The output of this effort is phase core output 2 (preparation of all needed inputs).

Disrupters (and Workarounds)

Three disrupters were identified for this effort, each related to trainers who are inadequate for the requirements of the effort.

- Trainers lack sufficient subject-matter expertise or training expertise.
  - The intuitive workaround for this is to deploy new trainers with the required expertise either by hiring them or by assigning a U.S. unit with a background in the subject.
- Trainers are insufficiently familiar with PN languages and customs. Depending on the circumstances, there could be several workarounds to this:
  - Contract interpreters with the necessary technical expertise.
  - Select trainers with previous expertise in country or in countries with similar cultures.
  - Conduct cultural familiarization training for U.S. personnel prior to engagement.

- Trainers are unfamiliar with goals and intent of the BPC effort.
  - An orientation should be conducted prior to engagement that ensures trainers understand U.S. goals and the broader context of U.S. assistance to the PN.

The U.S. Army's experiment with the new regionally aligned forces concept is an example of a disrupter in this area. While this concept promises to deploy tailored, trained, and consistently available Army units consisting of personnel with regional, cultural, and language capability,[7] interviews suggested that deployed personnel have yet to fully meet these expectations, lacking sufficient language and cultural skills. As a workaround in one case, in which personnel lacked language skills, the unit was augmented with interpreters who were familiar with PN language and cultural norms.

Equipment: Preengagement

Several specific inputs are required for equipment in the preengagement phase (Table 3.11). These inputs address not only the equipment itself but also its operation and maintenance. Since the role of equipment will vary from program to program, each of these inputs should be considered "if applicable." In each case, providing these inputs and transporting them to the training site constitute the activities associated with this phase.

The successful obtaining and provision of these inputs leads to five subordinate outputs from this phase and all these outputs contribute to the phase core output 1 (identification of needed inputs) and output 2 (preparation of needed inputs).

Disrupters (and Workarounds)

Identifying and providing equipment for a training event is a complex task. It is therefore not surprising that numerous disrupters may prevent accomplishment of the desired outputs in this phase (Table 3.12).

For some potential disrupters, the risk of injury, loss, or ineffective training is too high to allow training to proceed until they are addressed. Yet several of the workarounds are themselves showstoppers, delaying or stopping training until resolution. As with many lines of effort, the overarching recommendation is an early and constructive engagement with the PN to identify and address these issues promptly. In one case we considered, there was such a disconnect and lack of communication between those doing the training and those tasked with overseeing the training at a higher level that, when the latter ordered equipment, it was the wrong type of equipment and could not be used in the PN at all.

---

[7] "Regionally Aligned Forces and Global Engagement," presented to the Contemporary Military Forum III , 2013 AUSA Conference, October 18, 2013.

Table 3.11
Logic Model: Preengagement Phase of the Equipment Category

Specific Inputs	Activities	Disrupters (Activities–Outputs)	Workarounds (Activities–Outputs)	Subordinate Outputs—Ideal (Sufficient)	Category Phase Outputs Contribute to . . .
All U.S. stakeholders agree to the coordinated plan and performance measures	Synthesize equipment with the training plan	The United States and PN disagree on the role of equipment in the training program	Suspend activity and reengage appropriate decisionmakers	Coordination of an effective plan for use of equipment in training between United States and PN (U.S. and PN agreement on inclusion of equipment in the training program)	Phase core output 1, identification of all needed inputs
		PN does not believe the equipment is necessary or appropriate to the training			
		Sustainment is not part of the training curriculum	Revise curriculum and obtain PN approval		
Sufficient PN-provided equipment for training		PN does not release or diverts equipment prior to training	Suspend activity and reengage appropriate decisionmakers	(Identification of equipment appropriate for training prior to training)	
			Warehouse equipment in country in U.S. facilities and distribute as necessary		
			Loan U.S. equipment that will be returned at the completion of training		
Sufficient new or gifted equipment		Equipment procurement is not sufficient or differs from what the in-country team requested	Investigate relaxing of foreign military sales restrictions to boost PN inventory		
			Utilize assets lawfully seized from adversaries		
Service manuals (in the appropriate language)	Provide manuals for any equipment used or maintained during training (if required)	Manuals have not been written in the correct language or on a level PN personnel understand	Contract translation services and vendor to develop suitable manuals prior to event	(Supporting materials necessary for equipment utilization are on hand prior to training)	Phase core output 2, preparation of all needed inputs
		Manuals have not been cleared through the foreign disclosure or copyright process	—		
Ammunition for any live-fire exercises	Provide ammunition for live-fire exercises to be conducted during training (if required)	PN cannot provide ammunition and requires types not in the U.S. inventory	Contract a third party to provide ammunition		
		Ammunition is diverted from training, or PN personnel sell ammunition	Warehouse ammunition in country in U.S. facilities and distribute as needed		
Appropriate parts to maintain equipment throughout training cycle	Stock appropriate parts for equipment maintenance	PN cannot provide parts or requires parts not in U.S. inventory	Contract third party to provide parts	A maintenance plan and equipment parts are on hand	
		PN does not provide appropriate parts or diverts parts due to corruption			
A preventative maintenance plan for the equipment (cleaning, etc.)	Conduct common equipment maintenance	PN personnel are unaccustomed to or unwilling to perform daily maintenance actions	Include as requirement of training completion		
Communications equipment	Use communications gear to facilitate training and logistics	PN lacks sufficient gear	Provide U.S. equipment	Communications gear necessary for training is on hand prior to training	

Table 3.12
Disrupters and Workarounds: Preengagement Phase of the Equipment Input Category

Disrupters	Workarounds
The United States and PN disagree on the role of equipment in the training program	Suspend activity and reengage appropriate decisionmakers
PN does not believe the equipment is necessary or appropriate to the training	Suspend activity and reengage appropriate decisionmakers
Sustainment is not part of the training curriculum	Revise curriculum and obtain PN approval
PN does not release or diverts equipment prior to training	Suspend activity and reengage appropriate decisionmakers
	Warehouse equipment in country in U.S. facilities and distribute as necessary
	Loan U.S. equipment that will be returned at the completion of training
Equipment procurement is not sufficient or differs from what the in-country team requested	Investigate relaxing of foreign military sales restrictions to boost PN inventory
	Utilize assets lawfully seized from adversaries
Manuals have not been written in the correct language or on a level PN personnel understand[a]	Contract translation services and vendor to develop suitable manuals prior to event
Manuals not cleared through foreign disclosure or copyright process	Contract translation services and vendor to develop suitable manuals prior to event
PN cannot provide ammunition and requires types not in the U.S. inventory	Contract with third party to provide necessary materials; warehouse ammunition and parts and distribute as necessary for the event
Ammunition is diverted from training, or PN personnel sell ammunition	Warehouse ammunition in country in U.S. facilities and distribute as needed
PN cannot provide parts or requires parts not in U.S. inventory	Contract third party to provide parts
PN does not provide appropriate parts or diverts parts due to corruption	Contract third party to provide parts
PN personnel are unaccustomed to or unwilling to perform daily maintenance actions	Include as requirement of training completion
PN lacks sufficient gear	Provide U.S. equipment

[a] Note that this disrupter implicitly connects with the PN personnel input category, engagement phase, disrupter "Trainees lack literacy, aptitude, or physical conditioning for training" (see Table 2.8). There is an implicit tension to be balanced between manuals written to the language and literacy skills of ideal candidates and manuals written to lowest-common denominator trainee abilities.

Logistics and Transport: Preengagement

Numerous specific inputs are required to plan and implement a logistics effort (Table 3.13). First, *sufficient funding needs to be in place to resource the supplies and means of conveyance necessary* (this input is an output from the funding line of effort). Second, the actual *support to move personnel and equipment to the training facility* must be present. This may be contracted or provided from a nearby military unit. Third, replacement *parts must be on hand, and a maintenance plan must be in place to ensure that enough transport assets will be available.* Fuel must also be on hand.

Medical support, supplies, and transport are also inputs to this process. If not immediately available at the training location, a suitable facility must be identified or the capability must be provided through other means, such as additional U.S. personnel. Finally, a *means of transport and emergency response must be available for any U.S. trainers who will be in country.* In many countries, PN forces will cover this reliably, but

Table 3.13
Logic Model: Preengagement Phase of the Logistics and Transport Category

Specific Inputs	Activities	Disrupters (Activities–Outputs)	Workarounds (Activities–Outputs)	Subordinate Outputs—Ideal (Sufficient)	Category Phase Outputs Contribute to . . .
Sufficient program funding to resource all inputs and activities	Use funds to establish effective logistics effort	—	—	Resources available for logistics efforts in timely manner (Resources sufficient to ensure logistics support at various stages of program, such as prestage and trainee arrival, are on hand)	
Support necessary to move personnel and equipment to training facility	Move personnel and equipment	Infrastructure available for movement is inadequate (poor roads, etc.)	Consider alternative training location (including the possibility of third country)	(All or sufficient personnel and equipment are in place before start of training)	
			Evaluate cost of improving infrastructure to permit movement and staging		
		Customs or bureaucracy delays or impedes materiel delivery	Engage with PN officials and U.S. in-country team to ensure timely delivery		
		Transport resources are used for other purposes or missions (considered higher priority by PN)	Engage with PN counterparts on priority of transport		Phase core output 2, preparation of all needed inputs
			Consider providing U.S. transport assets		
Plan and parts on hand to maintain equipment	Establish a transport capacity and authorities to move repair parts	Infrastructure and transport resources are unavailable	Consider providing U.S. transport assets	Plan and parts are on hand to maintain equipment	
	Receive and store adequate fuel for the training cycle	Infrastructure and transport resources are unavailable	Consider providing U.S. transport assets	(Sufficient fuel is available for training)	
Means of transport and emergency response for U.S. trainers	Transport U.S. trainers; identify and prestage means of evacuation	It is difficult to move U.S. trainers to the training facility safely	Engage with PN officials to provide appropriate transport and remove delays	(U.S. personnel move safely to training location)	
		Extracting U.S. trainers in the event of natural disaster, security breach, etc., would be challenging	Coordinate with in-country team for appropriate force protection plans	(A viable plan exists for evacuating U.S. personnel in case of emergency)	
Medical personnel, supplies, and facilities	Ensure that appropriate medical personnel and supplies are on hand for all events	PN lacks adequate medical capabilities	Train medical personnel	Medical requirements have been satisfied prior to start of training (Medical personnel are on call and can respond within a reasonable time)	
			Stock from U.S. sources		

in others, the United States will want to obtain an independent means of transport in case of emergency.

These inputs enable such activities as moving personnel and equipment, establishing medical facilities, prestaging fuel, and developing an evacuation scenario for U.S. personnel that will be part of an overall force protection plan. The activities produce several subordinate outputs:

- Resources are available for logistics efforts in a timely manner.
- All (or sufficient number) of personnel are in place prior to commencement of training.
- Plan and parts are on hand to maintain equipment.
- Sufficient fuel is available for training.
- U.S. personnel are moved safely to training location.
- Viable plan exists to evacuate U.S. personnel in case of emergency.
- Medical requirements are satisfied prior to the start of training (in this case, this means having medical personnel on call and able to respond within a reasonable time throughout training).

Disrupters (and Workarounds)

In this line of effort and stage of the program, numerous issues can arise. Table 3.14 offers examples. Prior planning and ensuring some redundancy in capability are important steps to ensure the event can happen as scheduled.

Table 3.14
Disrupters and Workarounds: Preengagement Phase of the Logistics and Transport Input Category

Disrupters	Workarounds
Infrastructure available for movement is inadequate (poor roads, etc.)	Consider alternative training location (including the possibility of third country)
	Evaluate cost of improving infrastructure to permit movement and staging
Customs or bureaucracy delays or impedes materiel delivery	Engage with PN officials and U.S. in-country team to ensure timely delivery
Transport resources are used for other purposes or missions (considered higher priority by PN)	Engage with PN counterparts on priority of transport
	Consider providing U.S. transport assets
Infrastructure and transport resources are unavailable	Consider providing U.S. transport assets
Infrastructure and transport resources are unavailable	Consider providing U.S. transport assets
PN does not have adequate medical capability	Conduct training for medical personnel; stock supplies from U.S. sources
It is difficult to move U.S. trainers to the training facility safely	Engage with PN officials to provide appropriate transport and remove delays
Extracting U.S. trainers in the event of natural disaster, security breach, etc., would be challenging	Coordinate with in-country team for appropriate force protection plans
PN lacks adequate medical capabilities	Train medical personnel
	Stock from U.S. sources

Facilities: Preengagement

As with logistics, numerous specific inputs are required to begin preparing facilities for the BPC program (Table 3.15). The first two are outputs from previous lines of effort. *Identification of issues that need to be resolved prior to training* was an output from U.S. goals and plans and may involve a preengagement site survey with appropriate experts to determine what changes need to be made prior to the event. The *program being funded to a sufficient level* was an output from the funding line of effort and is required here because modifications to facilities may be costly.

There are three additional specific inputs. First, *information technology (IT) equipment and support that is appropriate for the training and for PN capabilities* are required. Second, *force protection measures* must be in place for U.S. personnel. Many of these measures involve facility configurations. Finally, a *full-time staff dedicated to operating the training facility* is required.

The activities in this phase center on making sure training facilities are adequate for use. Site surveys; identification of living quarters, if necessary; and formulation of a force protection plan will need to be conducted. Since any deficiencies must be addressed, funds may be utilized to refurbish facilities; changes may be made to support force protection requirements; and the United States may provide IT equipment, if the existing equipment is not sufficient. Finally, the staff required to operate the facility needs to be put in place if not already present.

These activities result in numerous subordinate outputs for this phase:

- identification of all facility-related issues that need to be resolved prior to training
- provision of adequate and secure quarters for all personnel prior to the start of training
- provision of space for training, with the minimum being sufficient space for lectures and administration
- preparation of field areas prior to the start of training
- establishment of adequate and reliable electrical supply prior to the start of training, with the minimum being an electrical infrastructure reliable enough to not impede training
- ensuring that resources are available for facilities in a timely manner
- ensuring that the necessary IT equipment is on hand and functioning prior to training
- ensuring that the facilities conform to U.S. force protection requirements
- effective manning and operation of the facility effectively throughout the program.

These outputs, with the exception of the identification of needed changes and facility staffing, form the inputs for the engagement phase. In this phase, they support phase

Table 3.15
Logic Model: Preengagement Phase of the Facilities Category

Specific Inputs	Activities	Disrupters (Activities–Outputs)	Workarounds (Activities–Outputs)	Subordinate Outputs— Ideal (Sufficient)	Category Phase Outputs Contribute to . . .
Identification of issues that need to be resolved prior to training	Survey facilities to be used throughout the training process (housing, training, medical, etc.) to determine suitability	PN is reluctant to provide access to examine facilities	Suspend activity and reengage appropriate decisionmakers	Identification of facility issues that need to be resolved prior to training	Phase core output 1, identification of all needed inputs
	Identify and evaluate living quarters for personnel	Current base facilities are inadequate for quarters	Contract to refurbish existing structures	(Adequate and secure quarters have been provided for all trainers and trainees prior to start of training)	Phase core output 2, preparation of all needed inputs
			Consider change of venue		
		Base does not meet force protection standards	House U.S. trainers at a separate location		
	Prepare adequate classroom and office space	Base lacks adequate functional space	Consider providing temporary, prefabricated buildings	Space is available that facilitates training (Space is available for lectures and administration)	
		PN does not provide adequate supplies (textbooks, smart boards, medical training aids, etc.)	Provide from U.S. sources		
	Prepare and maintain field areas appropriately for training	Field areas are in disrepair	Contract to prepare adequate areas	(Field areas have been prepared prior to start of training)	
		Base has insufficient field areas for training	Consider alternative training location		
	Provide adequate electricity for night and emergency operations	PN electrical grid is inadequate	Provide generators	An adequate and reliable electrical supply has been established prior to start of training (The electrical infrastructure is reliable enough not to impede training)	Phase core output 2, preparation of all needed inputs
		Base infrastructure does not support the electrical demand	Contract to improve base infrastructure		
Sufficient program funding to resource all inputs and activities	Detail facilities, including housing, in the program plan	PN officials are reluctant to have U.S. personnel living near the training facility	Investigate possibility of lodging U.S. personnel in embassy housing and transporting them to training daily	(Housing is adequate for the program and PN officials have agreed to allow U.S. trainers to use the housing)	
	Use funds to construct or refurbish appropriate training facilities	Military construction funds are not available or not permitted to be used for training	Consider augmenting PN funds with U.S. funds	(Resources are available for facilities in timely manner)	
IT equipment and support appropriate for PN capabilities	Provide U.S. or obtain PN IT equipment, if necessary	Base equipment and infrastructure are insufficient	Fund infrastructure improvements if possible; modify training curriculum to limit reliance on IT	(Necessary IT equipment is on hand and functioning prior to training)	Phase core output 2, preparation of all needed inputs
Security and force protection measures for U.S. personnel	Make physical changes to PN base; contract security guards; establish evacuation procedures	PN will not permit changes or procedures that would conform with force protection requirements	Suspend activity and reengage appropriate decisionmakers	(Facilities conform to U.S. force protection requirements)	
Full-time staff dedicated to operating training facility, if needed	Staff operating facility	PN is unwilling or unable to provide staff	Provide from U.S. sources for the duration of training	Facilities are effectively manned and operated throughout the program (Facility manning is sufficient to support the training program)	

core outputs 1 (identification of all needed inputs) and 2 (preparation of all needed inputs.

Disrupters (and Workarounds)

It should be expected that with so large an effort there would be numerous disrupters that prevent the achievement of the outputs (Table 3.16). Several of these disrupters are the result of poor facilities that are difficult to bring up to standards. Others are due to PN officials not being willing to work through planning or force-protection concerns.

Curriculum and Training Content: Preengagement

Formal standards for certification (or graduation) are a necessary input in the preengagement phase (Table 3.17). In this model, that is a subordinate output in the PN political will category, but agreement must be reached between U.S. and PN officials. An additional input may apply in some cases. *International standards for training* may be an important part of curriculum development if the BPC effort seeks to make PN forces capable and eligible to deploy in international or peacekeeping efforts.

The activities in this phase consist of *developing the curriculum based on the guidelines stakeholders have agreed to* and *synthesizing any required materials with the training*

Table 3.16
Disrupters and Workarounds: Preengagement Phase of the Facilities Input Category

Disrupters	Workarounds
PN is reluctant to provide access to examine facilities	Suspend activity and reengage appropriate decisionmakers
Current base facilities are inadequate for quarters	Contract to refurbish existing structures
	Consider change of venue
Base does not meet force protection standards	House U.S. trainers at a separate location
Base lacks adequate functional space	Consider providing temporary, prefabricated buildings
PN does not provide adequate supplies (textbooks, smart boards, medical training aids, etc.)	Provide from U.S. sources
Field areas are in disrepair	Contract to prepare adequate areas
Base has insufficient field areas for training	Consider alternative training location
PN electrical grid is inadequate	Provide generators
Base infrastructure does not support the electrical demand	Contract to improve base infrastructure
PN officials are reluctant to have U.S. personnel living near the training facility	Investigate possibility of lodging U.S. personnel in embassy housing and transporting them to training daily
Military construction funds are not available or not permitted to be used for training	Consider augmenting PN funds with U.S. funds
Base equipment and infrastructure are insufficient	Fund infrastructure improvements if possible; modify training curriculum to limit reliance on IT
PN will not permit changes or procedures that would conform with force protection requirements	Suspend activity and reengage appropriate decisionmakers
PN is unwilling or unable to provide staff	Provide from U.S. sources for the duration of training

Table 3.17
Logic Model: Preengagement Phase of the Curriculum and Training Content Category

Specific Inputs	Activities	Disrupters (Activities–Outputs)	Workarounds (Activities–Outputs)	Subordinate Outputs—Ideal (Sufficient)	Category Phase Outputs Contribute to . . .
Approved formal standards for certification of students	Develop curriculum that supports the attainment of standards	Standards are not likely to be attained within the allotted training time	Engage with PN counterparts to alter training time line or revisit standards	(The curriculum provides each trainee the opportunity to meet standards)	
		Curriculum does not follow a form familiar to PN trainees	Include PN counterparts in curriculum development		
		Standards have not been matched to the baseline proficiency of available PN trainees	Engage with PN counterparts to alter training time line, revisit standards, or designate different trainees		
	Synthesize materials with the training plan	U.S. and PN disagree on the utility of the instructional materials	Gain program acceptance from PN officials and establish communication channels for issues during program	All materials are in a language or dialect and at a technical level with which PN personnel will be comfortable (Materials sufficient match the language, dialect, and technical levels of trainees)	Phase core output 2, preparation of all needed inputs
International standards for training	Develop a curriculum that is in line with international standards (e.g., United Nations Department of Peacekeeping standards)	International standards are unattainable within allotted time and resources	Engage PN ministry on importance of meeting international standards, and revisit program goals if appropriate	The curriculum provides an opportunity for trainees and units to certify for international operations (Curriculum teaches capabilities necessary for international operations)	

plan. If international standards are applicable, *bringing the curriculum in line with the right set of standards* would be an additional activity. These activities seek to accomplish three subordinate outputs:

- a curriculum that provides the opportunity for each trainee to meet standards
- materials in a language or dialect and at technical level with which PN personnel will be comfortable
- a curriculum that provides an opportunity for trainees and units to certify for international operations if desired.

This realizes phase core output 2 (preparation of all needed inputs).

Disrupters (and Workarounds)

Despite the straightforward appearance of activities in the preengagement phase, several disrupters could have a detrimental effect on the training program if not mitigated (Table 3.18). Each of the workarounds for these disrupters involves engaging PN officials to revise agreements or address program shortfalls.

Table 3.18
Disrupters and Workarounds: Preengagement Phase of the Curriculum Input Category

Disrupters	Workarounds
Standards are not likely to be attained within the allotted training time	Engage with PN counterparts to alter training time line or revisit standards
Curriculum does not follow a form familiar to PN trainees	Include PN counterparts in curriculum development
Standards have not been matched to the baseline proficiency of available PN trainees	Engage with PN counterparts to alter training time line, revisit standards, or designate different trainees
U.S. and PN disagree on the utility of the instructional materials	Gain program acceptance from PN officials and establish communication channels for issues during program
International standards are unattainable within allotted time and resources	Engage PN ministry on importance of meeting international standards, and revisit program goals if appropriate

CHAPTER FOUR

Description of Logic Model Elements for the Engagement Phase

The engagement phase represented in the logic model is intended to be the period during which U.S. personnel are working directly with their PN counterparts to achieve the desired BPC outcome. Figure 2.1 showed this period as a "BPC event," with planning, coordination, resourcing, and assessment taking place before and after. This chapter details how the logic model was constructed to reflect actions taken during these individual events.

U.S. Program Goals and Plans: During Engagement

Goal alignment and planning are primarily the provenance of the preengagement phase. The outputs of the previous phase become the inputs to this phase (Table 4.1). This phase contains only three inputs in this category:

- the agreement of all U.S. stakeholders on a coordinated plan and performance measures
- identification of all supporting U.S. personnel and units
- making informed choices about departments and levels with which to engage.

These inputs support two activities. Both of these activities require other inputs to complete, and so will also appear in subsequent input categories:

- Conduct training according to the letter and spirit of U.S. and PN agreements.
- Engage PN personnel and conduct activities per the training plan.

These inputs and activities lead to two outputs, one concerning adherence to plans and the other concerning coordination and communication with the PN. Both outputs have two levels, "sufficient" and "ideal." This distinction also appears elsewhere in the model. The sufficient level is the minimum required for the logic of the logic model to remain intact and for the outputs to be sufficient to support subsequent

Table 4.1
Logic Model: Engagement Phase of the U.S. Goals and Plans Input Category

Specific Inputs	Activities	Disrupters (Activities–Outputs)	Workarounds (Activities–Outputs)	Subordinate Outputs—Ideal (Sufficient)	Category Phase Outputs Contribute to . . .
Coordinated plan and performance measures that all U.S. stakeholders agree with	Conduct training according to the letter and spirit of U.S. and PN agreements	U.S. or PN facilitators deviate from agreed-to plans	Supervise training with U.S. and PN representatives from in-country team and ministry	Training delivered is a product coordinated among U.S. and PN officials and meets the expectations of each (Training delivered is more or less as envisioned in program plan)	Phase core output 1, delivery of effective training
Identification of supporting U.S. personnel and units	Engage PN personnel and conducting activities per the training plan	An insufficient or excess number of U.S. personnel are assigned to cover PN interactions	Engage PN counterparts to adjust number of U.S. personnel during program if required	Continuous points of contact for U.S. and PN are sustained throughout the training process (Communication procedures and relationships established between PN and U.S. are sufficient to allow troubleshooting during training)	
Informed decisions about departments and levels with which to engage		Senior PN officials cannot be reached or engaged	Brief senior U.S. policymakers to discuss program in their interactions with PN counterparts		

desired outcomes. The ideal outputs are beneficial if not strictly required, but achieving them may make this BPC effort (or subsequent ones) go better and should be sought whenever possible.

Delivering training more or less in accordance with plans is an example of a sufficient output in this phase and input category. The ideal output, however, would be *delivering training as a coordinated product between U.S. and PN officials that meets the expectations of each.* Our research revealed that this can be a significant challenge. In one case, the United States and the PN had divergent expectations with respect to how and where to employ a newly established fixed-point border patrol unit. While the United States aimed to build a counterdrug unit focused on one border, the PN government tasked the unit to conduct expeditionary population security missions away from the border. The counterdrug priorities the government did have sat squarely at points of entry along a different border rather than on points of exit along the border of greater interest to the United States. If any lesson is to be learned, it is that successful BPC requires a negotiated compromise to ensure that U.S. and PN interests are mutually supportive and that the activities conducted meet expectations.

Similarly, regarding coordination and communication, the sufficient output is only that there be enough of a *communication procedure in place to troubleshoot any problems that arise during training.* Ideally, these connections would be both more than sufficient and more enduring.

These two subordinate outputs contribute to during engagement phase core output 1 (delivery of effective training).

Disrupters (and Workarounds)

The disrupters and workarounds for U.S. program goals and plans in the engagement phase center on executing the program in a manner that supports U.S. interests and staying engaged with PN officials to address any problems that may arise. Three disrupters and workarounds were identified:

- *U.S. or PN facilitators deviate from agreed-to plans.* This can lead to U.S. goals not being met despite conducting one or several events. One workaround for this might be to ensure that both U.S. in-country and PN ministerial teams supervise the training.
- *The number of U.S. personnel assigned is insufficient or in excess of what is needed to cover PN interactions.* In one case, the MILGP found itself limiting the number of U.S. personnel deploying to conduct BPC missions because the PN units did not have the absorption capacity (time or manpower to divert from ongoing security responsibilities) to receive additional training. If execution of the training program reveals that the number of U.S. personnel assigned is not optimal, PN officials should be engaged to adjust the number, if required.
- *An inability to reach or engage PN officials during the program.* The United States may not attain its goals if PN officials do not remain engaged throughout the process. In one country case we reviewed, U.S. officials recounted that, even in the midst of a joint training program, senior defense officials from the PN would leave the country for weeks at a time, during which there would be no communication. One potential remedy is to brief senior U.S. officials to mention or discuss the program during interactions with their PN counterparts to raise awareness and engagement.

U.S. Political Will: During Engagement

With the *program approvals* and *embassy support* from the preengagement phase carrying over as inputs, this phase focuses on ensuring the program is executed in a manner consistent with stakeholders' desires and keeping them informed on progress (Table 4.2). The first activity is *execution of the BPC program only within the bounds of the approvals.* While this seems straightforward, personnel conducting the BPC effort may run up against the bounds of approval in several ways. PN officials or trainees may be interested in material that is not in the curriculum; personnel or entities that have not been vetted or approved for training may attempt to join; or U.S. personnel may be invited to observe operations following training. For example, the United States granted Thailand's requests for replacement F-16s in the 1980s, but by the mid-1990s, the United States and Thailand seemed to have different goals for BPC. The United States thus declined to provide F/A-18s to the Thais, who then complained about a lack of access to the newest technologies. Moreover, some members of the Thai military elite

Table 4.2
Logic Model: Engagement Phase of the U.S. Political Will Category

Specific Inputs	Activities	Disrupters (Activities–Outputs)	Workarounds (Activities–Outputs)	Subordinate Outputs—Ideal (Sufficient)	Category Phase Outputs Contribute to . . .
Authorizations and approvals to execute mission	Execute BPC plan within bounds of approvals	Objectives or mission scope change	Embassy and/or CCMD monitor training program	Training conducted conforms to what senior U.S. officials desired from effort (Training is evaluated to have sufficiently conformed with training plan)	Phase core output 1, delivery of effective training
	Conduct BPC efforts with PN personnel and organizations to bring about desired U.S. results	Actual activities are restricted to subset of planned activities or interactions with specific PN entities	Identify larger numbers of candidate trainees from acceptable entities or organizations		
			Change training locations or types of training provided		Phase core output 3, training facilities, materials, and other resources adequately preserved for next use, cycle, or rotation
Embassy support for BPC efforts	Embassy officials remain engaged in training program throughout	Embassy officials focus on other efforts and are not involved once training begins	Schedule visits and observations by ambassador and other senior U.S. officials to keep spotlight on program and develop shared understanding		

felt that Thailand was being narrowly defined by capacity-building assistance in such areas as peacekeeping, disaster response preparation, and counterterrorism training.[1]

The second activity during engagement is *conducting BPC efforts with personnel and organizations that will bring about the desired results for U.S. stakeholders*. The program must be restricted to the personnel in units from the ministries, units, or regions identified as necessary and appropriate to supporting U.S. goals.

Finally, *U.S. officials must remain engaged throughout the process*. This may entail scheduling VIP visits during the course of instruction; arranging for embassy officials to observe the BPC effort; or, at least, providing regular status updates to the responsible in-country and CCMD officials. This effort to maintain U.S. stakeholder engagement makes it possible to respond more rapidly to any issues that may arise and allows a more efficient postevent assessment.

The output from this phase is that the *training conducted conforms to what senior U.S. officials desired from the effort*. Achievement of this output not only ensures that the current program is continued and resourced but also provides the foundation for developing follow-on efforts with the PN that U.S. officials will approve. This output contributes to the phase core outputs 1 (delivery of effective training) and 3 (adequate preservation of training facilities, materials, and other resources for next use, cycle, or rotation.

Disrupters (and Workarounds)

The model notes several possible disrupters, including

---

[1]   Lewis M. Stern, "Diverging Roads: 21st Century U.S.-Thai Defense Relations," *Strategic Forum*, No. 241, June 2009, p. 2.

- changing objectives or mission scope
- restriction of actual activities to a subset of planned activities or interactions with specific PN entities
- embassy officials focusing on other efforts and not being involved once training begins.

The model also includes several possible workarounds for these disrupters. Changing objectives can occur when original objectives have been met but vested interests keep the assistance going. For example, in one case, stakeholders described a situation in which contractors involved in certain aspects of BPC may have downplayed PN progress to ensure lucrative follow-on contracts. From the PN perspective, once capacity has been built, U.S. assistance presumably goes away, leading some PN units to underreport achievements to ensure the mission continues. Mission creep can also occur when the situation or the objectives change; when goals or objectives really change, such changes should be reflected in guidance, and BPC efforts should either be formally revised to correspond to the new mission or be supplemented with new efforts that will meet the expanding mission requirements. Mission creep might be avoided by monitoring activities at the CCMD or the embassy level. Restrictions on training or participants may require revising plans to focus on permissible training or to conduct training at different locations (if the restrictions are location based) or identifying larger numbers of trainee candidates from unrestricted PN organizations. Insufficient attention from the embassy might be corrected through reengagement or regular engagement with the embassy, by providing the ambassador opportunities for direct observation, or by eliciting engagement from other senior officials.

Partner Nation Political Will: During Engagement

The specific inputs for the engagement phase of this line of effort are made up entirely of the subordinate outputs from the preengagement phase (Table 4.3). The *program acceptance and lines of communication, an agreed-to set of events,* and *standards of certification* are all necessary to move to the engagement phase and each establishes a foundation for the BPC program effort. The only activity in this line of effort during the engagement itself is the *involvement of PN officials in the execution and monitoring of the effort.* Circumstances will dictate the nature of this involvement. In some programs, PN officers may be lead instructors. In other cases, involvement may be limited to visits from ministerial officials.

The *active involvement in the program* is itself a subordinate output of this phase. Experience has shown that keeping a focus on the BPC program, particularly a longer program, can be challenging. Two other subordinate outputs relate to PN officials' perceptions of the effort. The first output is *a belief among these officials that the training*

Table 4.3
Logic Model: Engagement Phase of the PN Political Will Category

Specific Inputs	Activities	Disrupters (Activities–Outputs)	Workarounds (Activities–Outputs)	Subordinate Outputs—Ideal (Sufficient)	Category Phase Outputs Contribute to . . .
—	—	PN counterparts change	Maintain frequent contact with PN officials to promote handoffs and joint briefings in the event of a change in personnel	—	—
Program acceptance from PN officials and establishment of communication channels for issues during program	PN officials are involved in planning, executing, and monitoring the program	PN officials focus on other efforts and are not involved once training begins	Schedule visits and observations by senior PN officials to keep spotlight on program	PN officials are actively involved throughout the training process (PN officials are kept informed of progress throughout program)	Phase core output 3, adequate preservation of training facilities, materials, and other resources for next use, cycle, or rotation
U.S. and PN agreement on an achievable set of training events				PN officials believe the training program is increasing their capacity (PN officials are receptive to continuing training efforts)	
Approval of formal standards for certification of students				PN officials believe certification of trainees is increasing PN capacity (PN officials are satisfied with trainee progress)	

program is increasing their capacity. This belief will likely be easier to achieve by keeping the officials engaged and up to date. The minimum version of this output is that the officials are receptive to continuing training or other BPC events. The second output is *a belief among partner officials that the certification of trainees is increasing their capacity.* More specifically, this output is that they recognize that their personnel are gaining important knowledge or skills from the process. The sufficient version of this output is that the officials are satisfied with trainee progress.

Each of these feeds phase core output 3 (adequate preservation of training facilities, materials, and other resources for next use, cycle, or rotation). As will be discussed in subsequent sections, the involvement of PN officials during the BPC program not only enhances the program but ensures that the groundwork is laid for future efforts.

Disrupters (and Workarounds)

Two disrupters were identified for this phase. The first is that the *PN officials are focused on other matters and not involved once the training begins.* As previously discussed, the involvement of PN officials not only gives legitimacy to the effort and enables prompt resolution of any issues but is also essential for planning follow-on efforts. The workaround that was identified for this was to schedule visits from U.S. officials of ranks corresponding to those of the PN officials involved and then extending invitations to the officials. If senior ministerial officials are not taking the opportunity to observe events, the U.S. ambassador inviting the officials to accompany him or her on a visit to training facilities might prompt participation.

The second disrupter is that the *PN counterparts change during the course of the program*, which may be very likely if the BPC effort spans several months or years. Maintaining regular communications with counterparts is the best workaround for this. Early knowledge of a change in personnel can facilitate handoff or joint briefings that may smooth the transition.

Funding: During Engagement

The funding effort during engagement is straightforward if no complications arise (Table 4.4). The specific inputs are the provided funds from both the United States and PN that were the outputs of the previous phase. The activity is to *fund the BPC effort according to any agreements that were reached between U.S. and PN officials.* Doing so effectively results in the subordinate output *of program activities being conducted with no stoppage or interruptions due to funding shortfalls.* This, in turn, supports phase core output 1 (delivery of effective training).

Disrupters (and Workarounds)
We identified five disrupters for this phase of the effort. Each is listed in Table 4.5 with one potential workaround.

Table 4.4
Logic Model: Engagement Phase of the Funding Category

Specific Inputs	Activities	Disrupters (Activities–Outputs)	Workarounds (Activities–Outputs)	Subordinate Outputs—Ideal (Sufficient)	Category Phase Outputs Contribute to . . .
Necessary funds to cover U.S. responsibilities in program	U.S. funds program activities	Projected U.S. funds are insufficient, and funding is used up prior to completion of program	Obtain program acceptance from PN officials and establish communication channels for issues during program	(Program activities are conducted with no stoppage or interruptions due to funding shortfalls)	Phase core output 1, delivery of effective training
		In-country team cannot redirect funds if problems arise	Appropriate funds so that in-country team has maximum flexibility		
		Funds do not carry into following fiscal years	Appropriate funds with two- or three-year money, if possible		
Necessary funds to cover PN responsibilities in program	PN funds program activities	PN funds are exhausted or halted due to instability or other reasons beyond counterparts' control	Supplement with additional U.S. funding		
		Resources are reallocated during program	Obtain program acceptance from PN officials and establish communication channels for issues during program		

Table 4.5
Disrupters and Workarounds: Engagement Phase of the Funding Input Category

Disrupters	Workarounds
Projected U.S. funds are insufficient, and funding is used up prior to completion of program	Obtain program acceptance from PN officials and establish communication channels for issues during program
In-country team cannot redirect funds if problems arise	Appropriate funds so that in-country team has maximum flexibility
Funds do not carry into following fiscal years	Appropriate funds with two- or three-year money, if possible
PN funds are exhausted or halted due to instability or other reasons beyond counterparts' control	Supplement with additional U.S. funding
Resources are reallocated during program	Obtain program acceptance from PN officials and establish communication channels for issues during program

The workarounds involving program acceptance from PN officials are outputs of the preengagement phase of PN political will. This speaks to the importance of engagement with PN officials and establishing channels of communication in resolving issues that arise during the course of training. The remaining workarounds center on the legal and bureaucratic mechanisms of fund allocation. In obtaining approvals from U.S. stakeholders, planners should attempt to build as much flexibility in fund allocation as possible into the program plan.

Partner Nation Personnel: During Engagement

Several specific inputs contribute to actions in the engagement phase regarding PN personnel (Table 4.6). The first is what will be an output in the logistics line of effort discussed later—that *all (or enough) personnel are in place prior to the start of training. Trainees having the necessary time, abilities, and willingness to train* are also specific inputs for this effort. Additionally, the *availability of maintenance and support personnel for the facilities* is an input (assuming the PN provides the personnel).

The support personnel would perform one activity in this phase: *fix equipment, operate ranges, maintain facilities, etc.* The other activity is simply *trainees attend and participate in training.* Both activities lead to the desired subordinate outputs for this phase. The first is that *training is run safely, and all equipment is in working order at the end of the BPC event* (the sufficient output being that insufficient maintenance does not impede training). The second output is that the *required number of trainees complete the program and achieve certification.* The second output doubles as phase core output 2 (required number of trainees complete the program and achieve certification). The other result of this effort is phase core output 1 (delivery of effective training).

Disrupters (and Workarounds)

As with the preengagement phase, we identified several critical disrupters and workarounds (Table 4.7). The workarounds for many of these disrupters involve engaging

Table 4.6
Logic Model: Engagement Phase of the PN Personnel Category

Specific Inputs	Activities	Disrupters (Activities–Outputs)	Workarounds (Activities–Outputs)	Subordinate Outputs—Ideal (Sufficient)	Category Phase Outputs Contribute to . . .
All (or sufficient) personnel in place prior to commencement of training	Trainees attend and participate in training	Inadequate infrastructure is available for movement (poor roads, etc.)	Reconsider training location; consider improvements to surrounding infrastructure, if practical.	(The required number of trainees completes the program and achieves certification)	Phase core output 2, required number of trainees complete the program and achieve certification
Willingness of trainees to train		PN personnel are not motivated to train	Engage with PN counterparts to reassign personnel		
Sufficient time to complete training		OPTEMPO restricts time available for training	Modify training plan; conduct less training or focus on "train the trainer"		
Trainees' availability to train		Trainee attention is lacking (distracted, high, fatigued, unauthorized absence, etc.)	Modify training plan (e.g., strict daily schedule)		
		PN trainees are not assigned in a timely manner	Engage with PN counterparts to ensure assignments		
		Trainees are unable to attend due to other duty requirements	Engage to have trainees assigned "PCS" or modify training schedule to accommodate PN personnel's other obligations		
Basic trainee skills		Trainees lack literacy, aptitude, or physical conditioning for training	Engage with appropriate PN counterparts to reassign personnel		Phase core output 1, delivery of effective training
			Adjust training program to train smaller number of qualified personnel		
Maintainers and support personnel for PN equipment and facilities	Fix equipment, manage ranges, etc.	PN does not provide sufficient support personnel	Contract an external provider	Training is run safely, and equipment is in working order at conclusion (Training not impeded by insufficient maintenance)	

PN counterparts to correct an issue, further underscoring the utility of establishing a path of communications prior to the beginning of the event.

Trainees may be absent for many reasons. In one of our case studies, a program had lower-than-expected attendance numbers because PN personnel were too busy conducting daily security responsibilities to take time out for additional training. As another example, U.S. trainers working with reconstituted Iraqi Army units frequently found unit strength to be at 60 to 75 percent during the training cycle.[2] One reason

---

[2]   U.S. Senate, Committee on Armed Services, *The Findings of the Iraqi Security Forces Independent Assessment Commission*, 110th Cong., 1st sess., September 6, 2007, p. 65.

Table 4.7
Disrupters and Workarounds: Engagement Phase of the PN Personnel Input Category

Disrupters	Workarounds
Inadequate infrastructure is available for movement (poor roads, etc.)	Reconsider training location; consider improvements to surrounding infrastructure, if practical.
PN personnel are not motivated to train	Engage with PN counterparts to reassign personnel
OPTEMPO restricts time available for training	Modify training plan; conduct less training or focus on "train the trainer"
Trainee attention is lacking (distracted, high, fatigued, unauthorized absence, etc.)	Modify training plan (e.g., strict daily schedule)
PN trainees are not assigned in a timely manner	Engage with PN counterparts to ensure assignments
Trainees are unable to attend due to other duty requirements	Engage to have trainees assigned "PCS" or modify training schedule to accommodate PN personnel's other obligations
Trainees lack literacy, aptitude, or physical conditioning for training	Engage with appropriate PN counterparts to reassign personnel
	Adjust training program to train smaller number of qualified personnel
PN does not provide sufficient adequate support personnel	Contract an external provider

for this was that Iraqi soldiers were paid in cash by the Ministry of Defense. Lacking an electronic banking system or other means of delivering payments directly to their homes, many soldiers were forced to hand-carry large amounts of money home on a regular basis—thus risking their safety and contributing to rampant absenteeism from their units.

U.S. Trainers: During Engagement

Trainers who are knowledgeable in the subject matter and effective at delivering training and who are *in place at the commencement of training* are the specific inputs for the engagement phase (Table 4.8). There is only one activity for this phase. The *trainers conduct the event per the plan the U.S. and PN officials agreed to.* If successful, there will be two subordinate outputs. The first will be *the U.S. trainers impart information to the trainees effectively.* The second will be the *training conducted addresses the major objectives of the program.* Both support core phase objective 1, effective training delivered.

Disrupters (and Workarounds)

The disrupters involved in the engagement phase are issues with which many who have coordinated training events are familiar (Table 4.9). They cover ineffective instruction and a lack of credibility between instructors and students. As with workarounds in numerous other phases, the solutions to these disrupters are based on a high amount of engagement with PN officials and attention to the training program during its execution.

One additional disrupter is entirely internal to U.S. personnel. Much of the success of the long-term BPC effort depends on an accurate and objective assessment of

Table 4.8
Logic Model: Engagement Phase of the U.S. Trainers Category

Specific Inputs	Activities	Disrupters (Activities–Outputs)	Workarounds (Activities–Outputs)	Subordinate Outputs—Ideal (Sufficient)	Category Phase Outputs Contribute to . . .
Trainers who are knowledgeable on subject matter and able to communicate material effectively to trainees	U.S. trainers conduct program per plan	Trainers are not communicating with PN personnel effectively	Review contracted translator performance, trainer qualifications, or cultural training for effectiveness	(U.S. trainers effective in communicating information contained in training plan)	Phase core output 1, delivery of effective training
		Trainers deviate from plan	U.S. program personnel and embassy team monitor course	(Training conducted that addresses major objectives of the program)	
		PN trainees do not respect the trainers due to rank or civilian status	Pair trainers with PN cadre that will be present in classes, share office space, etc.	—	
—		U.S. personnel manipulate assessments (inflated to exaggerate accomplishments or deflated to keep training effort going)	Embassy and/or CCMD monitors training program	—	
All (or sufficient) personnel in place before training starts		PN officials, commanders, or students do not see U.S. trainers as credible or trustworthy	Arrange for third party (allied nation, regional partner, contractors with experience) to participate or take the lead in training	—	

Table 4.9
Disrupters and Workarounds: Engagement Phase of the U.S. Trainers Input Category

Disrupters	Workarounds
Trainers are not communicating with PN personnel effectively	Review contracted translator performance, trainer qualifications, or cultural training for effectiveness
Trainers deviate from plan	U.S. program personnel and embassy team monitor course
PN trainees to not respect the trainers due to rank or civilian status	Pair trainers with PN cadre that will be present in classes, share office space, etc.
U.S. personnel manipulate assessments (inflated to exaggerate accomplishments or deflated to keep training effort going)	Embassy and/or CCMD monitors training program
PN officials, commanders, or students do not see U.S. trainers as credible or trustworthy	Arrange for third party (allied nation, regional partner, contractors with experience) to participate or take the lead in training

the program itself. Some U.S. stakeholders may have an incentive to skew the program assessment. This may be to exaggerate their own accomplishments or to ensure that the training effort continues (as in the case mentioned under "U.S. Political Will: Engagement." In either case, the workaround for this disrupter is for personnel not directly involved in the event, presumably from the U.S. embassy or the CCMD, to closely monitor the training program.

Equipment: During Engagement

Having any *necessary equipment, parts, documentation, and communications gear on hand* are inputs to the engagement phase (Table 4.10). The activities of this phase will depend largely on the nature of the training, but it is safe to assume they center on familiarizing trainees with the equipment and service manuals, conducting exercises,

Table 4.10
Logic Model: Engagement Phase of the Equipment Category

Specific Inputs	Activities	Disrupters (Activities–Outputs)	Workarounds (Activities–Outputs)	Subordinate Outputs—Ideal (Sufficient)	Category Phase Outputs Contribute to . . .
An effective plan for use of equipment in training coordinated between the United States and PN	Familiarize PN personnel with new equipment, applications, and sustainment	PN personnel lack the capacity to learn how to use new equipment	Modify training plan to build capacity prior to introducing new equipment	Training program integrates classroom and "hands on" activities	Phase core output 1, delivery of effective training
All (or sufficient) equipment in place prior commencement of training			Adjust training certification standards	As necessary, PN personnel gain proficiency in equipment maintenance and operation	
—		—	—	—	Phase core output 2, required number of trainees complete the program and achieve certification
Supporting materials for equipment utilization are on hand prior to training	Familiarize PN personnel with service manuals	PN operators do not have a culture of using publications	Use service manuals as training materials	PN personnel utilize service manuals for upkeep and operation of equipment (PN maintenance practices informed by publications)	Phase core output 3, training facilities, materials, and other resources adequately preserved for next use, cycle, or rotation
	Conduct live-fire exercises to reinforce training goals (if required)	PN personnel are not sufficiently familiar with equipment to conduct safe firing exercises	Modify training plan to conduct firing exercises later in curriculum or at follow-on event	All exercises necessary for accomplishment of training goals are conducted	
		Range facilities do not exist to facilitate safe firing exercises	Identify issues that need to be resolved prior to training		
A maintenance plan and equipment parts are on hand prior to training	Maintain equipment during the course of training.	PN lacks appropriate personnel for maintenance	Include training for PN maintainers in the training plan	All (or reasonable proportion of) equipment remains in service	
	Draw parts from stock to maintain equipment	PN logistics approval process is insufficient	Program acceptance by PN officials and establishment of communication channels for issues during program		
Communications gear necessary for training is on hand prior to training	Use communications gear for training and for managing the training program	PN communications are not secure	Institute frequency-hopping and other methods to protect unencrypted communications	Effective communications for both U.S. and PN personnel (Communications capability sufficient for running training program)	

maintaining the equipment, and utilizing communications gear as part of the training or to aid in facilitating the program.

If executed effectively, the engagement phase results in several subordinate outputs.

- The training program integrates classroom and "hands on" activities.
- PN personnel gain proficiency in equipment maintenance and operation.
- PN personnel use service manuals for upkeep and operation of equipment (a sufficient output is that such publications inform PN maintenance practices).
- All exercises necessary for the attainment of training objectives are completed.
- All (or a reasonable portion of) the equipment remains in service.
- Communications are effective for both U.S. and PN personnel (a sufficient output would be a communications capability adequate for running the training program).

Indicative of the importance of equipment to the training cycle, these subordinate outputs contribute to all three core phase outputs: 1 (delivery of effective training), 2 (required number of trainees complete the program and achieve certification), and 3 (adequate preservation of training facilities, materials, and other resources for next use, cycle, or rotation).

Disrupters (and Workarounds)

Numerous disrupters may prevent achievement of the phase outputs (Table 4.11). These disrupters may represent sensitive aspects of the BPC effort, since the majority of them pertain to a lack of PN capability, and several involve institutional cultures, changes that may be difficult to advocate.

Table 4.11
Disrupters and Workarounds: Engagement Phase of the Equipment Input Category

Disrupters	Workarounds
PN personnel lack capacity to learn how to utilize new equipment	Modify training plan to build capacity prior to introducing new equipment
	Adjust training certification standards
PN operators do not have a culture of using publications	Use service manuals as training materials
PN personnel are not sufficiently familiar with equipment to conduct safe firing exercises	Modify training plan to conduct firing exercises later in curriculum or at follow-on event
Range facilities do not exist to facilitate safe firing exercises	Identify issues that need to be resolved prior to training
PN lacks appropriate personnel for maintenance	Include training for PN maintainers in the training plan
PN logistics approval process is insufficient	Program acceptance by PN officials and establishment of communication channels for issues during program
PN communications are not secure	Institute frequency-hopping and other methods to protect unencrypted communications

Logistics and Transport: During Engagement

Each of the subordinate outputs of the preengagement phase is carried over as an input to the engagement phase (Table 4.12). If these are carried over successfully, little activity occurs in this phase other than *continuing to logistically support the program, utilize assets as required for training, maintain the ability to move U.S. personnel in case of emergency, and ensure proper medical care is provided.*

These activities lead to five subordinate outputs:

- Logistics assets are managed to support training activities.
- All (or a reasonable proportion of) the equipment remains in service.
- U.S. personnel move safely and efficiently.
- Means to evacuate U.S. personnel are available.

Table 4.12
Logic Model: Engagement Phase of the Logistics and Transport Category

Specific Inputs	Activities	Disrupters (Activities–Outputs)	Workarounds (Activities–Outputs)	Subordinate Outputs—Ideal (Sufficient)	Category Phase Outputs Contribute to . . .
Resources available for logistics efforts in timely manner	Coordinate with PN officials to support training program	PN officials lack sufficient logistics assets throughout training cycle	PN officials accept program; communication channels are set up to address issues during program	Logistics assets are managed to support training activities	Phase core output 1, delivery of effective training
Plan and parts to maintain equipment on hand prior to training	Use parts to perform required maintenance throughout training cycle	Authorities for permitting release of parts and fuel are inadequate	PN officials accept program; communication channels are set up to address issues during program	All (or reasonable proportion of) equipment remains in service	Phase core output 3, training facilities, materials, and other resources are adequately preserved for next use, cycle, or rotation
Sufficient fuel available for training	Use fuel to keep vehicles operational throughout training cycle	PN corruption leads to poor fuel quality	—		
U.S. personnel can move to training location safely	Establish rules and methods for moving U.S. personnel	PN laws do not support the U.S. training mission and status of trainers (weapons carried, activities)	Agree to status of U.S. group prior to team entering country	U.S. personnel move safely and efficiently	
A viable plan for evacuating U.S. personnel in case of emergency	Maintain ability to evacuate U.S. personnel	—	—	Means to evacuate U.S. personnel	Phase core output 2, required number of trainees completes the program and achieves certification
Medical requirements have been satisfied prior to start of training	Meet all emergent and routine medical needs of participants	Medical personnel not aware of training demands and disqualify trainees unnecessarily or clear them inappropriately	Brief U.S. or PN medical personnel on training regimen prior to event	Urgent and routine medical needs of training participants are addressed promptly throughout program (Personnel attrition due to medical reasons kept to a minimum)	

- Urgent and routine medical needs of training participants are addressed promptly throughout the program (this is also an output of the facilities line of effort; a sufficient output is minimization of personnel attrition for medical reasons).

The goal of the engagement phase for logistics and transport is the realization of two core phase outputs: 2 (required number of trainees complete the program and achieve certification) and 3 (adequate preservation of training facilities, materials, and other resources for next use, cycle, or rotation).

Disrupters (and Workarounds)

Most of the disrupters for this phase involve a lack of PN support; one pertains to the training of medical personnel (Table 4.13). Although the workarounds are as specific as possible, these disrupters will all likely require engagement and negotiation with PN officials.

For example, we received an anecdote regarding one country case in which helicopter training and operations were suspended due to the corrupt sale of high-quality aviation fuel and its replacement with lower-quality fuel. This problem was (eventually) resolved through patience and careful and diplomatic engagement with the commander of the relevant PN formation.

Facilities: During Engagement

Once the event begins, the facilities should not be a major coordination concern (Table 4.14). In this phase, the facilities are utilized and maintained. Several subordinate outputs are desirable in in this phase:

- Personnel are housed in appropriate conditions.
- U.S. personnel are housed in a secure location throughout the training cycle.

Table 4.13
Disrupters and Workarounds: Engagement Phase of the Logistics and Transport Input Category

Disrupters	Workarounds
PN officials lack sufficient logistics assets throughout training cycle	PN officials accept program; communication channels are set up to address issues during program
Authorities for permitting release of parts and fuel are inadequate	PN officials accept program; communication channels are set up to address issues during program
PN corruption leads to poor fuel quality	—
PN laws do not support the U.S. training mission and status of trainers (weapons carried, activities)	Agree to status of U.S. group prior to team entering country
Medical personnel not aware of training demands and disqualify trainees unnecessarily or clear them inappropriately	Brief U.S. or PN medical personnel on training regimen prior to event

Table 4.14
Logic Model: Engagement Phase of the Facilities Category

Specific Inputs	Activities	Disrupters (Activities–Outputs)	Workarounds (Activities–Outputs)	Subordinate Outputs—Ideal (Sufficient)	Category Phase Outputs Contribute to . . .
Adequate and secure quarters for all trainers and trainees prior to start of training	House trainees in quarters	PN personnel do not show the ability or inclination to maintain living quarters	Contract U.S. personnel to conduct maintenance Obtain program acceptance from PN officials and establish communication channels for issues during program	Personnel are housed in appropriate conditions	Phase core output 1, delivery of effective training
	House U.S. personnel in an area that complies with force protection requirements	Training facility conditions necessitate housing U.S. personnel at a separate location	Engage U.S. special operations forces (which have fewer force protection requirements) to conduct training	U.S. personnel housed in secure location throughout training cycle	
Classroom space that facilitates training	Use space for training and administration	PN personnel do not show ability or inclination to maintain classrooms	Contract U.S. personnel to conduct maintenance Obtain program acceptance from PN officials and establish communication channels for issues during program	Classrooms that effectively facilitate training (Training areas sufficient for class instruction)	Phase core output 3, training facilities, materials, and other resources are adequately preserved for next use, cycle, or rotation
Field areas prepared prior to start of training	Use training areas for field exercises	PN personnel do not show the ability or inclination to maintain field areas	Contract U.S. personnel to conduct maintenance Obtain program acceptance from PN officials and establish communication channels for issues during program	Field areas that effectively facilitate training (Field areas sufficient for conducting exercises)	
Adequate and reliable electrical supply is established prior to start of training	Provide electrical power for all facilities	PN personnel do not show the ability or inclination to maintain electrical equipment	Contract U.S. personnel to conduct maintenance Obtain program acceptance from PN officials and establish communication channels for issues during program	Equipment and facilities powered throughout training cycle (Training not impeded by electrical infrastructure)	Phase core output 1, delivery of effective training
Resources are available for facilities in timely manner	Coordinate with PN officials to support training program	PN does not maintain facilities throughout the training cycle	Obtain program acceptance from PN officials and establish communication channels for issues during program	Facilities are managed to support training activities	
Necessary IT equipment on hand and functioning prior to training	Use IT effectively to support training	The PN infrastructure does not support IT systems	Provide infrastructure prior to training	IT equipment that effectively augments instruction (IT equipment utilized in training program)	Phase core output 1, delivery of effective training
Facilities conform to U.S. force protection requirements	Ensure U.S. personnel remain within approved facilities throughout training cycle	Force protection requirements are not sufficient or cannot be achieved	Reconsider training location	U.S. personnel comply with FP requirements	

- Classrooms and field areas effectively facilitate training (the sufficient output is that classrooms and field areas are adequate for training).
- Equipment and facilities arepowered throughout training cycle (the sufficient output is that the electrical infrastructure does not impede training.
- Facilities are managed to support training activities.
- The IT equipment effectively augments instruction.
- U.S. personnel comply with force protection requirements.

In addition to these outputs, these efforts realize the phase core outputs 1 (delivery of effective training) and 3 (adequate preservation of training facilities, materials, and other resources for next use, cycle, or rotation).

Disrupters (and Workarounds)

The disrupters that were identified for the engagement phase may be politically sensitive to address (Table 4.15). Many of them involve PN personnel being unable or unwilling to maintain facilities in some form. But due to the cost and effort involved in construction or refurbishment, U.S. officials may find it necessary to press their counterparts for better performance to keep the facilities available for future use.

Curriculum and Training Content: During Engagement

The three outputs from the preengagement phase are the inputs for the engagement phase (Table 4.16). In this phase, the activities are straightforward: *Training is conducted according to the curriculum; materials are utilized to enhance training; and international operational standards are addressed and made a priority, if appropriate.* Each of the inputs leads to a corresponding subordinate output:

- The curriculum is verified as being effective in achieving PN and U.S. goals.
- The training materials augment instruction effectively.
- The curriculum achieves standards for international operations effectively.

Table 4.15
Disrupters and Workarounds: Engagement Phase of the Facilities Input Category

Disrupters	Workarounds
PN personnel do not show ability or inclination to maintain living quarters	Contract U.S. personnel to conduct maintenance; establishment of communication channels for issues during program (PN political will)
Training facility conditions necessitate housing U.S. personnel at separate location	Engage U.S. special operations forces (SOF) to conduct training (SOF may have fewer force protection requirements)
PN personnel do not show ability or inclination to maintain classrooms, field areas, or electrical equipment	Contract U.S. personnel to conduct maintenance; establishment of communication channels for issues during program (PN political will)
PN infrastructure does not support IT systems	Provide infrastructure though U.S. resources prior to training
Force protection requirements are not sufficient or cannot be achieved	Reconsider training location

Table 4.16
Logic Model: Engagement Phase of the Curriculum and Training Content Category

Specific Inputs	Activities	Disrupters (Activities–Outputs)	Workarounds (Activities–Outputs)	Subordinate Outputs—Ideal (Sufficient)	Category Phase Outputs Contribute to . . .
The curriculum provides each trainee the opportunity to meet standards	Train to curriculum	The curriculum is insufficient to achieve standards	Obtain program acceptance from PN officials and establish communication channels for issues during program	Curriculum verified as effective in achieving PN and U.S. goals (Curriculum supports U.S. and PN BPC goals)	Phase core output 2, required number of trainees completes the program and achieves certification
All materials are in a language or dialect and at a technical level with which PN personnel will be comfortable	Use materials to enhance training	PN personnel assigned to training are not literate	Ensure that sufficient PN personnel with appropriate qualifications are present at facility prior to commencing training	Training materials that effectively augment instruction (Training materials utilized in instruction)	
The curriculum provides an opportunity for trainees and units to certify for international operations	Train to standards for international operations	PN policy does not permit deployment for international operations	Revisit training to determine whether it is cost-effective if international operations are not going to be supported	Curriculum verified as effective in achieving standards for international operations (Training objectives met support international operations)	

In total, this phase produces output 2 (required number of trainees complete the program and achieve certification).

Disrupters (and Workarounds)

Three disrupters would inhibit progress in this phase. First, *the curriculum could be found to be ineffective in achieving standards.* In this case, the communication channels established between U.S. and PN officials would likely need to be used to make quick and sweeping changes to the curriculum. Second, a *lack of literacy among PN trainees* would slow down training immensely if the curriculum used printed materials. Here, too, there is no fix U.S. officials can apply unilaterally. PN officials will need to be consulted to either modify the training or provide new personnel. Finally, the *partner government may be against deploying for peacekeeping operations.* In this case, the curriculum should be assessed to determine what topics are geared toward international standards and how they can be deleted or modified.

CHAPTER FIVE

Description of Logic Model Elements for the Postengagement Phase, Including Outcomes

This chapter highlights the elements of the logic model that pertain to the postengagement phase—the phase in which the BPC event is assessed for effectiveness and in which the efforts made during the event are carried forward through additional training, operations, or maintenance. As with the engagement phase, the logic model addresses the postengagement phase that is tied to each BPC event rather than the BPC program as a whole.

U.S. Program Goals and Plans: Postengagement

The postengagement phase for the U.S. program goals and plans input category (Table 5.1) has only two inputs, one an output from the preengagement phase and one an output from the engagement phase:

- a coordinated plan and performance measures that all U.S. stakeholders agree on
- continuous points of contact for the United States and the PN throughout the training process.

These two inputs support two activities:

- establishing capabilities and institutions that will ensure program has longevity
- maintaining contacts with PN officials to ensure program effects are continued.

The inputs and activities contribute to a single subordinate phase output, which relates to PN political will, which is its own input category. The ideal version of that output is *procedures are established for continuing dialogue and future training opportunities*; the sufficient version is just that *communication on future efforts continues with the PN*. This output contributes to phase core output 2 (continuing maintenance and sustainment of new forces and equipment, training facilities, and materials).

Table 5.1
Logic Model: Postengagement Phase of the U.S. Goals and Plans Input Category

Specific Inputs	Activities	Disrupters (Activities–Outputs)	Workarounds (Activities–Outputs)	Subordinate Outputs—Ideal (Sufficient)	Category Phase Outputs Contribute to . . .
Agreement of all U.S. stakeholders on a coordinated plan and performance measures	Establish capabilities and institutions that will ensure program longevity	PN shows no interest or ability in sustaining program results	Include sustainment and program improvement measures as part of the coordinated plan	Procedures are established for continuing dialogue and future training opportunities (Communication on future efforts continues)	Phase core output 2, continuing maintenance and sustainment of new forces and equipment, training facilities and materials
Continuous U.S. and PN points of contact throughout training process	Maintain contacts with PN officials to ensure program effects continued	U.S. and PN officials rotate to other assignments	Establish a regular schedule for PN meetings so visibility on rotations is maintained and "hand-offs" occur		

Disrupters (and Workarounds)

The logic model includes two possible disrupters, one for each input-activity pair. The first is *PN shows no interest or ability in sustaining program results.* This would be difficult to work around, but progress might be made by including sustainment and program improvement measures in the coordinated plan. The second is a *break in lines of communication caused by U.S. and PN officials rotating to other assignments.* Because rotations on both sides are inevitable, care should be taken to protect connections and contacts by institutionalizing regular meetings, maintaining visibility on rotations, and taking care in transitions and handovers.

U.S. Program Goals and Plans: Outcomes

If all the temporal phases successfully produce all their intermediate phase outputs, the U.S. program goals and plans input category should produce four outcomes (Table 5.2):

- The executed plans effectively increase partner capacity in desired areas and consistent with U.S. BPC goals.
- U.S. stakeholders accept and support the executed plans.
- Plans enable future engagement and continued incremental progress toward U.S. BPC goals.
- Relationships and connections are sufficient to support future engagement and progress toward U.S. BPC goals.

These four outcomes contribute significantly to two of the three high-level BPC training and equipping outcomes that are the ultimate outcomes of the overall model, 1 (capacity built), and 3 (PN relationship).

Table 5.2
Logic Model: Outcomes of the U.S. Goals and Plans Input Category

Outcomes and Consequences			Subordinate Outcomes	Highest Level Outcome Category Contributed to . . .
Disrupters (Outputs–Outcomes)	**Workarounds (Outputs–Outcomes)**	**Possible Unintended Consequences**		
Stakeholders continue to argue for modifications to BPC plan	Identify the lead group for pursuing the BPC plan in consultation with embassy team	—	U.S. stakeholders accept and support executed plans	1. Capacity is built: Capable units are formed and equipped in accordance with objectives
U.S. goals unrealistic in terms of capability improvement or time required	Break plan into increments by fiscal year and establish review procedures to ensure standards are being met and training is appropriate	PN officials do not feel they have a say in influencing the plan. They go through the motions or reject it.	Executed plans effectively increase partner capacity in desired areas and are consistent with U.S. BPC goals	
—	—	—	Plans enable future engagement and incremental progress toward U.S. BPC goals	3. The relationship with the PN continues: Relationships are created or preserved, making further security cooperation possible
U.S. approach to PN officials coordinated poorly. Officials are approached out of sequence or not by the correct U.S. stakeholder	Designate the embassy team as message coordinators	—	Relationships and connections are sufficient to support future engagement and progress toward BPC goals	

Disrupters (and Workarounds)

Three possible disrupters might prevent the sequential phase outcomes from generating these outputs. Table 5.3 presents these and candidate workarounds.

For example, in an early period of BPC engagement in Colombia (~1990–1999), what were first unrealistic goals with respect to the initial time line for countering the dual threats of violent drug trafficking organizations and insurgent groups were mollified by the extended time line accompanying Plan Colombia (first funded in 2000), a multiyear effort backed by generous funding that was ultimately successful in achieving several top U.S. program goals in that country.[1]

U.S. Political Will: Postengagement

The postengagement phase for this line of effort focuses on assessing the results of the BPC program and briefing them to U.S. stakeholders (Table 5.4). This assessment should evaluate not only the BPC program itself but any indications that PN capacity has increased in the desired ways. The assessment should be framed in terms of metrics that were used in the program development and, if appropriate, should also include a cost analysis of BPC activities and "next steps" in the effort.

---

[1]   DeShazo, Primiani, and McLean, 2007.

Table 5.3
Disrupters and Workarounds: Outcomes Phase of the U.S. Program Goals and Plans Input Category

Disrupters	Workarounds
Stakeholders continue to argue for modifications to BPC plan	Identify the lead group for pursuing the BPC plan in consultation with embassy team
U.S. goals unrealistic in terms of capability improvement or time required	Break plan into increments by fiscal year and establish review procedures to ensure standards are being met and training is appropriate
U.S. approach to PN officials coordinated poorly. Officials are approached out of sequence or not by the correct U.S. stakeholder	Designate the embassy team as message coordinators

Table 5.4
Logic Model: Postengagement Phase of the U.S. Political Will Category

Specific Inputs	Activities	Disrupters (Activities–Outputs)	Workarounds (Activities–Outputs)	Subordinate Outputs—Ideal (Sufficient)	Category Phase Outputs Contribute to . . .
Training that conforms to what senior U.S. officials desired from the effort	Conduct postprogram assessment using agreed-to metrics and brief senior U.S. officials on state of PN capabilities and continuing efforts	Accusations of additional human rights or other abuses occur	Maintain U.S. presence to monitor PN operations or consider suspension of assistance	U.S. BPC efforts in PN are "good news stories" that create opportunity for further efforts (U.S. officials open to considering further efforts)	Phase core output 3, continuing maintenance and sustainment of necessary relationships between and across U.S. and PN elements
		Loss of momentum after original training event		Efforts lead to enriched and continued engagement with PN officials (Dialogue with PN officials continues)	

The first output from this phase is that *the BPC efforts are "good news stories" that U.S. officials can use as examples of constructive cooperation.* The sufficient output in this case is that *U.S. officials are open to continuing the engagement.* This may be the only attainable output if U.S. efforts were not public or if the training effort encountered significant problems.

The second output from this phase is *enriched engagement between the United States and PN stakeholders.* The results of the BPC effort may extend beyond the building of the specific capacity through a deepening relationship with PN officials or the establishment of trust between the United States and the PN. The sufficient version of this output is *continuing dialogue with PN officials*, which may not be a deepening of the relationship but at least results in further discussions. Each of these supports the phase core output 3 (continuing maintenance and sustainment of necessary relationships between and across U.S. and PN elements).

Disrupters (and Workarounds)

One disrupter identified for this phase is likely to be at the forefront of U.S. stakeholders' concerns throughout the process: Is the new PN capacity used in a way that is detrimental to U.S. goals or values? One example of this is *U.S.-trained PN personnel conducting human rights abuses or being accused of such actions.* This has (unfortunately) happened repeatedly in the last decade. The United States has been unable to collaborate unreservedly with several PNs that have inconsistent records on human rights.

The second disrupter is *loss of momentum following the training event*. While the first iteration of an effort may have the attention of senior U.S. and PN officials, subsequent efforts may be seen as routine. The training regimen could suffer through scheduling delays or selection of participants that are not up to the original standards. Thus, although the original event was a success, the prospects for furthering the relationship and achieving U.S. goals are diminished over time. In several U.S. Pacific Command countries, coups or attempted coups have led the United States to suspend aid and put BPC programs on hold, sometimes for extended periods.

The workaround for both of these disrupters is continued U.S. engagement and monitoring (end-use monitoring is a statutory requirement for most equipment transfers or sales). The means and level of effort required for the follow-on U.S. engagement should be briefed to U.S. stakeholders as part of the initial planning process. But a continuing working-level interaction would assist in spotting abuses early and keep the spotlight on the BPC effort. Failing this, suspending assistance should be considered if U.S. officials no longer feel that the PN is acting responsibly or that the United States is getting a return on its investment of resources.

U.S. Political Will: Outcomes

The outcome of efforts involving U.S. political will is that *the BPC effort enjoys the support of U.S. officials* (Table 5.5). This support will, at the very least, be private but, if appropriate, could be very public and very central to the relationship between the two countries. The wide range of potential U.S. stakeholders is indicative of the importance of ensuring BPC efforts are nested within the broader U.S. engagement in the country and region. It is also indicative of the potential benefits of an effective engagement both in development of PN capacity and the development of the political and defense relationship. This subordinate outcome contributes to high-level outcome 3 (relationships).

Table 5.5
Logic Model: Outcomes of the U.S. Political Will Category

Outcomes and Consequences				
Disrupters (Outputs–Outcomes)	Workarounds (Outputs–Outcomes)	Possible Unintended Consequences	Subordinate Outcomes	Hightest Level Outcome Category Contributed to . . .
Political fallout comes from greater U.S. role in PN security	Maintain secrecy (or at least discretion) in U.S. presence and efforts	—	BPC program enjoys the support (private and public if possible) of U.S. officials	3. The relationship with the PN continues: Relationships are created or preserved, making further security cooperation possible

Disrupters (and Workarounds)

One disrupter for this line of effort was that a *greater U.S. role or presence in PN security may have political fallout.* For example, public reaction in the United States to Egypt's recent political turmoil and violent military crackdown has affected U.S. decision-makers' views on whether to curb the longstanding and largely successful military-to-military relationship that has provided Egypt billions of dollars of military assistance.[2] Despite total satisfaction in program accomplishment among U.S. stakeholders, the relationships that are so key to this effort may still be negatively affected by the effort itself.

One possible workaround to this issue is to maintain secrecy, or at the very least discretion, in the effort. The training can take place exclusively within the confines of a PN base, in an isolated location, or even in a third country; and U.S. officials can maintain a low-key presence, if possible. This may give PN officials the flexibility they need in downplaying the U.S. role in development of their capacity.

Partner Nation Political Will: Postengagement

Each of the outputs from the engagement phase is also an input for the postengagement phase, with one addition (Table 5.6). The preengagement output that *the program satisfies both U.S. and PN objectives* is also a specific input to this phase. The themes of this phase are assessing the utility of the BPC effort and planning future engagements. The model specifies four activities.

First, *a review of the training program should be conducted with PN officials and a discussion should begin about whether the desired objectives were met.* Second, *another discussion should cover whether the program should be repeated or expanded on.* Part of this discussion, if appropriate, should be the areas in which the PN can begin to assume responsibility. Depending on the topic and circumstances, students from the first iteration can be instructors for the second, or PN personnel can take over certain aspects of the training. Third, any *follow-on training or "reachback" should be discussed.* Particularly when new equipment is the focus of training, PN officials should be aware of the extent to which program participants are able to contact trainers or companies and receive assistance in the future. Finally, a *broader discussion (hopefully a continuation of*

---

[2]   The United States has provided significant military aid to Egypt since 1970, including $1.3 billion a year in from 1987 to the present (Jeremy M. Sharp, "Egypt: Background and U.S. Relations," Congressional Research Service, June 5, 2014). An August 2013 Pew Research survey found that a slim majority (51 percent) of Americans felt the United States should cut military aid to Egypt (Bruce Drake, "Curbing Military Aid to Egypt Has Support Among the U.S. Public," Washington, D.C.: Pew Research Center, October 9, 2013). More recently, one nongovernmental organization report noted that, "a number of observers, including many U.S. democracy and human rights advocates, argue that U.S. military support for Egypt runs counter to U.S. security interests and/or democratic values" (see Project on Middle East Democracy, "Working Group on Egypt Releases Letter to President Obama," February 3, 2014).

Table 5.6
Logic Model: Postengagement Phase of the PN Political Will Category

Specific Inputs	Activities	Disrupters (Activities–Outputs)	Workarounds (Activities–Outputs)	Subordinate Outputs—Ideal (Sufficient)	Category Phase Outputs Contribute to ...
A program plan that satisfies both U.S. and PN requirements	Review training program with PN officials and discuss objectives	—	—	PN officials consider the program a success in meeting objectives (PN officials open to considering further efforts)	Phase core output 3, continuing maintenance and sustainment of necessary relationships between and across U.S. and PN elements
Active involvement of PN officials throughout the training process	Discuss repetition of training and areas where PN can assume responsibility	PN officials content to permit continued U.S. handling of functions that PN could perform	Outline "scaling back" of U.S. involvement with each interaction of training Build institutionalized training cadre through train-the-trainer efforts that can become self-sustaining	Steps are taken to make ongoing efforts as indigenous as possible (PN takes ownership of some aspects of future training)	Phase core output 2, continuing maintenance and sustainment of new forces and equipment, training facilities, and materials
PN officials believe the training program is increasing their capacity	Discuss follow-on training and technical reachback capability	—	—	Procedures are established for continuing dialogue and future training opportunities (Communication on future efforts continues)	
PN officials believe certification of trainees is increasing PN capacity	Discuss areas where training will benefit PN operations	No indication that PN officials plan to change operations or utilize trainees as intended (or according to U.S. objectives)	Maintain U.S. presence to monitor PN operations and consider suspension of assistance, renegotiation of program, or shifting of effort to other units	PN officials take steps to incorporate increased capacity in planning for future operations (PN officials recognize increased capacity)	Phase core output 3, continuing maintenance and sustainment of necessary relationships between and across U.S. and PN elements

a discussion) on the areas in which the training will benefit operations should take place. This is an opportunity for U.S. officials to reaffirm that the PN intends to use the new capacity in the manner the United States intended when developing the BPC plan.

We identified four subordinate outputs (Table 5.7) for this phase of PN political will, corresponding to two of the core outputs for the postengagement phase. These outputs center on consolidating the improvement in capacity by establishing communication channels and future opportunities.

Disrupters (and Workarounds)

We identified two disrupters for this phase. The first is that, moving forward, *PN officials are content to let the United States handle functions of the program that partner forces could handle.* This may be acceptable to U.S. officials under some circumstances, such as when the continued effort also provides continued access. But in an era of tightening budgets, we can assume that, if any effort can be "indigenized," it is in the interests of the United States that it should be. Efforts toward this end are under way in Bangladesh, where the United States is helping to train an already capable Bangla-

Table 5.7
Phase and Core Outputs from Postengagement Phase of the PN Political Will Input Category

Subordinate Outputs	Phase Core Outputs
PN officials consider the program a success in meeting objectives	Phase core output 3, continuing maintenance and sustainment of necessary relationships between and across U.S. and PN elements
Steps are taken to make ongoing efforts as indigenous as possible	Phase core output 2, continuing maintenance and sustainment of new forces and equipment, training facilities, and materials
Procedures are established for continuing dialogue and future training opportunities	Phase core output 2, continuing maintenance and sustainment of new forces and equipment, training facilities, and materials
PN officials take steps to incorporate increased capacity in planning for future operations	Phase core output 3, continuing maintenance and sustainment of necessary relationships between and across U.S. and PN elements

deshi peacekeeping force into a model for the region, with the ultimate goal of helping Dhaka stand up a first-rate train-the-trainer program to support peacekeeping training for other nations.[3] We found two workarounds: The first is for U.S. officials to outline the "scaling back" of U.S. involvement during postengagement discussions with their counterparts. The second is to focus initial efforts on establishing an institutionalized "training cadre" of PN personnel who will be responsible for follow-on events, possibly with U.S. assistance.

The second disrupter is significant for BPC efforts: *PN officials not indicating a willingness to change their operations or utilize the trainees as intended.* This has happened in at least two ways. The first is intentional and follows mismatched goals: If the PN believes that one security threat has a higher priority than the one that is of interest to the United States, forces trained for the latter (say, counternacotics) may be used for the former (perhaps internal security or counterinsurgency). A second disrupter is less intentional: We considered one case in which individuals received specialized training but then rotated away from their units and never returned to a posting in which the training was relevant.

Such disconnects should not be likely if sufficient discussions took place prior to the BPC program. However, it is a scenario that would significantly affect the ability to move forward because U.S. policymakers are unlikely to approve continued efforts with unpredictable results. The workaround to this is to maintain a U.S. presence or an ability to track PN operations and employment of personnel. If U.S. goals are not being met following the BPC program, U.S. officials should consider suspending assistance or shifting resources to focus on other units.

Partner Nation Political Will: Outcomes

As with U.S. political will, one subordinate outcome of this line of effort is that *BPC efforts enjoy the support of PN policymakers* (Table 5.8). If necessary, the support of poli-

---

[3]   Dan Mozena, U.S. Ambassador to Bangladesh, "America's Partnership with Bangladesh National Defense College Mirpur," remarks, Dhaka, Bangladesh: Embassy of the United States of America, August 5, 2013

Table 5.8
Logic Model Outcomes for the PN Political Will Category

Outcomes and Consequences				
Disrupters (Outputs–Outcomes)	Workarounds (Outputs–Outcomes)	Possible Unintended Consequences	Subordinate Outcomes	Hightest Level Outcome Category Contributed to . . .
PN officials are too quick to believe U.S. involvement is no longer required	Promote enriched and continued engagement with PN officials	—	BPC program enjoys the support (private and public if possible) of PN officials	3. The relationship with the PN continues: Relationships are created or preserved, making further security cooperation
PN does not allocate resources to continue training		—		
PN does not follow through on sustainment training and plans		—		
—		—	PN confidence in its ability to conduct operations increases	
—	—	—	PN officials are open to continued engagement and follow-up actions	

cymakers can be muted or even private, depending on the political ramifications of U.S. assistance. We identified two other subordinate outcomes: an *increased confidence on the part of the PN to conduct operations utilizing their increased capacity* and *PN officials being open to continued engagement with their U.S. counterparts* and the pursuit of beneficial follow-up actions.

Disrupters (and Workarounds)

We identified three disrupters that prevent realization of these outcomes. First, *PN officials may be too quick to determine that U.S. assistance is no longer required.* Second, *PN officials may not allocate the needed resources to continue these efforts* after an initial period. Finally, *the PN may not follow through on sustainment, subsequent training, or other plans.* The workaround for each of these is an output from the postengagement phase of U.S. political will. In that phase, we identified "enriched engagement with PN officials" as an output. Each of the disrupters in this phase would best be mitigated by a close and honest interaction between U.S. and PN officials.

Funding: Postengagement

The only specific input to the postengagement phase of funding is the output of an uninterrupted program from the previous phase (Table 5.9). The activity at this stage is to *conduct a review of the training program with PN officials.* As with other lines of effort, the aim in this phase is to build toward future engagement opportunities. The subordinate output is that both *U.S. and PN officials consider the program a success* (and hence, wise allocation of funds). This supports the phase core output 3 (continuing

Table 5.9
Logic Model: Postengagement Phase of the Funding Category

Specific Inputs	Activities	Disrupters (Activities–Outputs)	Workarounds (Activities–Outputs)	Subordinate Outputs—Ideal (Sufficient)	Category Phase Outputs Contribute to . . .
Program activities that are conducted with no stoppage or shortfalls due to funding	Review training program with PN officials and discuss objectives	Disagreement on resourcing sustainment funding Disagreement over cognizant U.S. agency for funding sustainment	Plan U.S. side of sustainment phase prior to initiating BPC program	U.S. and PN officials consider the program a success in meeting objectives	Phase core output 3, continuing maintenance and sustainment of necessary relationships between and across U.S. and PN elements

maintenance and sustainment of necessary relationships between and across U.S. and PN elements).

Two disrupters were identified for this line of effort, both relating to U.S. program support. The first is a disagreement about the source of funding for sustainment of the new capability. Training and equipment "bought" with money from one budget cycle may need to be resourced from subsequent cycles. The second is determining which U.S. agency is responsible for funding (and monitoring) the PN's new capacity moving forward. U.S. planners should address each of these potential disrupters in the initial program phases.

Funding: Outcomes

The subordinate outcome of the funding line of effort is intuitive—*the program is funded to a level sufficient to resource all inputs and activities.*

Partner Nation Personnel: Postengagement

Both phase outputs from the engagement phase are inputs in the postengagement phase (Table 5.10). The required number of trainees achieving certification leads to three activities in the postengagement phase. First, *billets requiring the certification must be identified or established.* This means that the trainees must be eligible to fill certain billets based on their training. Second, the *PN units that will be exercising new capabilities must be established or identified.* These may be units that conducted training as a group. If not, new authorities or the assignment of training graduates to specific units may be required. Third, the *new skills or capacity must be applied to real-world operations.* It is difficult to claim that PN capacity has been increased if the focus of the training was rare or unrealistic operations. The second specific input is that *training is conducted and equipment is in working order.* This leads to the activity of *maintaining equipment and continuing to apply safe training practices* in the postengagement phase.

Table 5.10
Logic Model: Postengagement Phase of the PN Personnel Category

Specific Inputs	Activities	Disrupters (Activities– Outputs)	Workarounds (Activities– Outputs)	Subordinate Outputs—Ideal (Sufficient)	Category Phase Outputs Contribute to . . .
The required number of trainees completes the program and achieves certification	Establish or identify billets requiring completion of training	Trained personnel not used as intended (not assigned to take advantage of training received)	PN officials open to continued engagement and follow-up actions	Graduates are assigned to skill-relevant positions	Phase core output 1, trained (and equipped) personnel are used to form and man units, augment existing units, or train others (as specified in objectives)
	Establish or identify units that will be exercising new PN capabilities	Trained personnel not used as intended (not assigned to appropriate unit)		Graduates are assigned to new or augmented units	
	Apply new skills to real-world operations	Training insufficient to permit intended operations	Modify training curriculum for next iteration	A cadre of program graduates has been assigned to positions and units that have responsibility for intended operations (Program graduates are retained)	
		Poor retention of PN personnel following training does not permit PN forces to increase force capability	Retention bonuses for trained PN personnel		
Training is run safely, and equipment is in working order at the conclusion	PN personnel maintain equipment and continue to apply safe training practices	Maintenance and training standards not maintained	PN officials open to continued engagement and follow-up actions	Equipment and training standards utilized in further efforts (Increase in PN awareness of maintenance and training standards)	Phase core output 2, continuing maintenance and sustainment of new forces and equipment, training facilities, and materials

The outputs of this phase follow the activities closely. The first output is that *certified graduates of the training are assigned to positions relevant to their skills.* If applicable, the second output is that these *trainees are utilized in new or augmented units that will be exercising the new capacity.* The final output is a *cadre of program graduates in positions and units that have responsibility for the operations intended by U.S. goals* (the sufficient output being that program graduates are retained in the PN's service). The final output carries the input of operable equipment forward. Specifically, it is that *equipment and training standards are utilized in future efforts* (the sufficient output being an increase in PN awareness of maintenance and training standards). The outputs support two of the phase core outputs for postengagement: 1 (trained and equipped personnel are used to form and man units, augment existing units, or train others) and 2 (continuing maintenance and sustainment of new forces and equipment, training facilities, and materials).

Disrupters (and Workarounds)

The disrupters for this phase concern ineffective use of program graduates and effects of training that are not sustained. Two disrupters are very similar and involve not assigning training graduates as intended, the first focusing on the billet assigned and the second on not being assigned to an appropriate unit. In both cases the workaround is engagement with partner officials to determine what measures need to be taken to assign graduates appropriately. The third disrupter is that the *training is actually insuf-*

ficient to permit the PN to undertake the intended operations. This requires reviewing the training curriculum to determine whether iteration would provide additional capability. Another disrupter was *poor retention of personnel,* which could be especially problematic if the partner military typically has high turnover or if the training provides a useful skill for the civilian sector. One workaround is similar to one employed in the United States, offering retention bonuses to training graduates. The final disrupter is *PN personnel not adhering to maintenance and training standards after conclusion of the event.* This circumstance would need to be addressed with PN officials prior to follow-on engagements.

Such disrupters are not confined to challenging contexts but are more common as contextual challenges mount. *Jane's* reported that the time line for certain Romanian reforms slipped due to insufficient funding for modernization and restructuring. Funding limitations were also linked to training and equipment readiness shortfalls; the Romanian Chief of Staff noted in 2002 that, because only 15 percent of the required fuel was available, 70 percent of pilots had insufficient flying time, and only one-half of ships had actually left port.[4] Such challenges persisted despite the Romanian government's decision to increase its Ministry of Defense's budget by 30 percent (an effort to approach North Atlantic Treaty Organization averages) in 2001.

Partner Nation Personnel: Outcomes

The subordinate outcome of the PN personnel line of effort is that the *required numbers of personnel are trained and man units, conduct operations, or train others* (Table 5.11). This outcome supports two of the broad outcomes of the model: outcome 1 (capable units have been formed and equipped in accordance with objectives) and outcome 2 (maintenance and sustainment are occurring, and training capability is being preserved).

One disrupter was identified in the outcomes for PN personnel: the PN creating special units to receive the training, equipment, etc., but then disbanding the units after the event in an effort to "spread the wealth." While it may be reasonable from the PN perspective, this will disrupt the effort to ensure program sustainment.

U.S. Trainers: Postengagement

As with other lines of effort, the focus of this postengagement phase is setting the stage for follow-on actions or a repetition of training (Table 5.12). The outputs from the engagement phase, *effective communication by trainers* and *training that addresses pro-*

---

[4] Jane's Information Group, "Romania, Armed Forces," *Jane's Country and Military Assessments,* November 7, 2002.

Table 5.11
Logic Model Outcomes for the PN Personnel Category

Outcomes and Consequences				
Disrupters (Outputs–Outcomes)	**Workarounds (Outputs–Outcomes)**	**Possible Unintended Consequences**	**Subordinate Outcomes**	**Hightest Level Outcome Category Contributed to . . .**
—	—	Program is overemphasized, and PN assigns personnel and pursues training at the expense of more-attainable improvements	The required personnel have been trained to man units, conduct operations, or train others	1. Capacity is built: Capable units are formed and equipped in accordance with objectives
PN created temporary composite units to receive training and equipment (and spread resources across PN stakeholders), then disbands them	PN officials are open to continued engagement and follow-up actions	—		
—	—	Trainees conduct human rights abuses		
—	—	U.S.-trained personnel become a threat to the PN government (coup)		
—	—	—		2. Capacity is sustained: Maintenance and sustainment are occurring, and a training capability has been preserved (or institutionalized)

Table 5.12
Logic Model: Postengagement Phase of the U.S. Trainers Category

Specific Inputs	**Activities**	**Disrupters (Activities–Outputs)**	**Workarounds (Activities–Outputs)**	**Subordinate Outputs—Ideal (Sufficient)**	**Category Phase Outputs Contribute to . . .**
U.S. trainers effectively communicate information contained in training plan	Conduct AAR of program to determine areas for improvement and possibility for greater PN involvement	Trainers do not conduct AARs	Make AARs required for each training activity	Reports from each training event that evaluate effectiveness (General assessment of training program that evaluates effectiveness)	Phase core output 2, continuing maintenance and sustainment of new forces and equipment, training facilities, and materials
		PN officials do not conduct course evaluations	Invite outside group (ex: DPKO) to monitor training and provide feedback	Assessment of training effectiveness from those outside the planning process	
The training conducted addresses the major objectives of the program	Establish long-term solution for delivery of training or indigenization	Third party trainers not able to commit to involvement in future iterations	Focus on training the trainer and quickly building indigenous training capacity	Modification to training plan that facilitates future PN use	Phase core output 3, continuing maintenance and sustainment of necessary relationships between and across U.S. and PN elements

gram objectives, are inputs to this phase that feed two key activities. The first is the *conduct of an after-action review (AAR) of the program* to determine areas for improvement and areas where the PN could have a greater (or lead) role in the future. The second key activity *is establishment of a long-term solution for delivery of training or indigenization,* assuming further effort is required and desired by both parties.

These activities lead to three subordinate outputs:

- reports from each training event that evaluate effectiveness (the sufficient output is a general assessment of the training program that evaluates effectiveness)
- assessment of training effectiveness from outside the planning process
- modifications to the training plan that facilitate future PN use.

These efforts address phase core outputs 2 (continuing maintenance and sustainment of new forces and equipment, training facilities, and materials) and 3 (continuing maintenance and sustainment of necessary relationships between and across U.S. and PN elements).

U.S. Trainers: Outcomes

The subordinate outcome for this effort is that *U.S. trainers improve PN capabilities through training conducted effectively and appropriately* (Table 5.13). Achievement of this output supports high-level outcome 1 (capacity is built).

Disrupters (and Workarounds)

We identified one disrupter: *The assistance from the United States, including the presence and leading role of U.S. trainers, may become a political problem for the PN* and negate the impact of the training. Thus, despite an effectively conducted training event, the PN may not take steps to increase its capacity and may not be open to future BPC efforts.

This disrupter may be mitigated by maintaining discretion in conducting the program. This might entail U.S. trainers remaining on base, not publicly acknowledging the program or issuing press releases, or taking other steps to keep the U.S. presence low key.

Table 5.13
Logic Model: Outcomes for the U.S. Trainers Category

Outcomes and Consequences				
Disrupters (Outputs– Outcomes)	**Workarounds (Outputs– Outcomes)**	**Possible Unintended Consequences**	**Subordinate Outcomes**	**Hightest Level Outcome Category Contributed to . . .**
Improved relations with U.S. become a political problem for PN	Maintain discretion in conducting program (U.S. trainers remain on base, no public acknowledgment, etc.)	—	U.S. trainers improve PN capabilities through training that is conducted effectively and appropriately, in accordance with the training plan	1. Capacity is built: Capable units are formed and equipped in accordance with objectives

Equipment: Postengagement

Utilizing the specific inputs that come from the engagement phase, activities in postengagement focus on assessing the use of equipment in the training program and possibly turning equipment over to the PN (Table 5.14). Parts may be turned over, or contracted support may be arranged to build or replenish the PN's stock. Each of the activities focuses on ensuring the PN integrates new knowledge, equipment, or practices into its future training or operations. We identified six subordinate outputs the postengagement phase:

Table 5.14
Logic Model: Postengagement Phase of the Equipment Category

Specific Inputs	Activities	Disrupters (Activities–Outputs)	Workarounds (Activities–Outputs)	Subordinate Outputs—Ideal (Sufficient)	Category Phase Outputs Contribute to . . .
Training program integrates classroom and "hands on" activities	Assist PN trainers in developing programs that utilize available equipment	PN is reluctant to "waste" equipment operations on training	Provide the program additional equipment that is intended to be used for training only	PN integrates equipment into continuing training pipeline	Phase core output 1, trained (and equipped) personnel are used to form and man units, augment existing units, or train others (as specified in objectives)
As necessary, PN personnel gain proficiency in equipment maintenance and operation	Turn equipment over to PN personnel	PN personnel are not allowed to use new equipment after completing training	PN officials become open to continued engagement and follow-up actions	PN integrates equipment into operations	
		PN personnel do not choose to use new equipment after completing training			
		Equipment is diverted after training			
PN personnel utilize service manuals for upkeep and operation of equipment	PN personnel continue to utilize manuals and technical publications	PN personnel are not accustomed to consulting manuals and following procedures	PN officials become open to continued engagement and follow-up actions	A library of technical publications is available to PN personnel	Phase core output 2, continuing maintenance and sustainment of new forces and equipment, training facilities, and materials
All exercises necessary for accomplishment of training goals are conducted	PN personnel become proficient in safe conduct of live-fire exercises without U.S. assistance	—	—	PN incorporates effective safety procedures and practices in live-fire events (Awareness of safety protocols for live-fire events increases)	
	Fully turn over maintenance and operation of live-fire facilities	—	—	Live-fire range facilities to support future training are maintained for future use (Live-fire ranges are available for future training with only minimal restoration)	
All (or a reasonable proportion of) equipment remains in service	PN personnel establish and maintain proficiency at preventative and corrective maintenance	PN does not keep up preventative maintenance practices	PN officials become open to continued engagement and follow-up actions	PN personnel conduct effective maintenance procedures	—
	Utilize parts remaining to stock PN supplies	PN does not establish parts release procedures or loses parts to corruption			—

- The PN integrates equipment into a continuing training pipeline.
- The PN integrates equipment into its operations.
- A library of technical publications is available to PN personnel.
- The PN incorporates effective safety procedures and practices in live-fire events. Live-fire range facilities are maintained for future use.
- PN personnel follow effective maintenance procedures.

Related to these are phase core outputs 1 (trained and equipped personnel are used to form and man units, augment existing units, or train others) and 2 (continuing maintenance and sustainment of new forces and equipment, training facilities, and materials).

Disrupters (and Workarounds)

The maintenance and sustainment of U.S.-provided equipment is particularly challenging. We are aware of numerous examples of equipment not being maintained after receipt that was thus lost to service at a rate much higher than expected. Lack of maintenance can stem from many sources, among them lack of proclivity to conduct maintenance, lack of needed tools and spares, and lack of instruction on maintenance for specific equipment. For example, in Senegal, an insufficient investment in sustainment has led to deterioration, as "the state of Senegalese military equipment has been found to be in need of improvement," and "[t]here are problems of obsolescence and poor serviceability in the existing inventory, and the [defense] budget is too restricted to redress this situation."[5]

Equipment: Outcomes

Although the only overall outcome addressed is "capable units formed and equipped in accordance with objectives," there are several subordinate outcomes for the equipment line of effort (Table 5.15):

- PN personnel use their own equipment with greater effectiveness.
- The PN integrates new equipment into operations.
- The PN builds a culture of procedural and manual compliance.
- Live-fire exercises become a part of PN training plans.
- PN personnel develop a culture of preventative maintenance.
- Effective communications facilitate training, security, and logistics.

---

[5] Jane's Information Group, "Procurement: Senegal," *Jane's Military and Security Assessments*, October 13, 2011.

Table 5.15
Logic Model: Outcomes of the Equipment Category

Subordinate Outcomes	Hightest Level Outcome Category Contributed to . . .
PN personnel use own equipment more effectively	
PN integrates new equipment into operations	
PN builds culture of procedural and manual compliance	Phase core output 1, trained (and equipped) personnel are used to form and man units, augment existing units, or train others (as specified in objectives)
Live-fire exercises become a part of PN training plans	
PN personnel develop culture of preventative maintenance	
Training, security, and logistics are facilitated by effective communications	

These outcomes represent an increase in partner capacity not just within individuals or units but also in the partner's ability to formulate and effectively conduct training evolutions.

Logistics and Transportation: Postengagement

Other than the normal AAR process, there is very little to be done in the logistics line of effort postengagement (Table 5.16). One specific activity is to *encourage PN planners to include medical support when developing future training events, if that need has not previously been addressed.* The planning for and provision of this support is the phase's only subordinate output and supports phase core output 2 (continuing maintenance and sustainment of new forces and equipment, training facilities, and materials).

Logistics and Transportation: Outcomes

That *PN logistics processes are exercised and improved* is a subordinate outcome of the line of effort if applicable in a specific case (Table 5.17). Some BPC efforts may not require support from the PN; in other cases, the partner's logistics ability may be nearly proficient. But in many cases, an improvement in logistics capacity is a beneficial corollary to the greater BPC effort. The second outcome for this line of effort is the *establishment of medical support for training events and a reduction in the number of trainees who attrite for medical reasons.*

Facilities: Postengagement

The housing, training areas, and infrastructure maintained through the BPC event become the specific inputs for the postengagement phase (Table 5.18). As with other lines of effort, the focus of this phase is to ensure the ability to carry this effort over

Table 5.16
Logic Model: Postengagement Phase of the Logistics and Transport Category

Specific Inputs	Activities	Disrupters (Activities–Outputs)	Workarounds (Activities–Outputs)	Subordinate Outputs—Ideal (Sufficient)	Category Phase Outputs Contribute to . . .
Minimal personnel attrition for medical reasons	PN planners include medical support in developing follow-on training activities	—	—	Medical support is provided in future PN training events (Increased PN awareness of the importance of medical support)	Phase core output 2, continuing maintenance and sustainment of new forces and equipment, training facilities, and materials

Table 5.17
Logic Model: Outcomes of the Logistics and Transport Category

Subordinate Outcomes	Highest Level Outcome Category Contributed to . . .
PN logistics processes exercised and improved	2. Capacity is sustained: Maintenance and sustainment are occurring, and a training capability has been preserved (or institutionalized)
PN builds medical capabilities by including medical support in training plans	

to future training events. The activities involve *maintaining the facilities, housing, and IT systems and utilizing them after the event*. These lead to five intuitive subordinate outputs:

- Housing facilities remain available for future events.
- Quarters are available for U.S. personnel involved in future training iterations.
- Facilities are available to the PN for future training events.
- The power grid remains in service.
- IT systems remain available for future use.

It should be clear from the nature of these outputs that they serve phase core output 2 (continuing maintenance and sustainment of new forces and equipment, training facilities, and materials).

Disrupters (and Workarounds)

Each disrupters in this section pertains to PN management of facilities following a BPC event. One disrupter specifically interferes with permitting future U.S. training to take place: the PN modifying the facilities to the point where they are no longer compliant with U.S. force protection or other requirements. The workaround for this is straightforward—PN officials must be made aware that future U.S. involvement will depend on facility standards being maintained.

A second noteworthy disrupter is that the maintenance of facilities depends on a model of contractor support. This approach may be intuitive and familiar for U.S. personnel, but the PN officials charged with facility maintenance may be inexperienced with such an approach or may face a bureaucracy with more barriers to contracting than in the United States. The workaround for this disrupter is to fashion a sustain-

Table 5.18
Logic Model: Postengagement Phase of the Facilities Category

Specific Inputs	Activities	Disrupters (Activities–Outputs)	Workarounds (Activities–Outputs)	Subordinate Outputs—Ideal (Sufficient)	Category Phase Outputs Contribute to . . .
Personnel are housed in appropriate conditions	Housing facilities remain in use and to standards	—	—	Housing facilities remain available for use for future events	Phase core output 2, continuing maintenance and sustainment of new forces and equipment, training facilities, and materials
U.S. personnel are housed in a secure location throughout the training cycle	Housing facilities remain in compliance with force protection standards	PN modifies facilities after U.S. departure (if located on PN base)	Inform PN counterparts that future U.S. involvement will depend on meeting force protection requirements	Quarters are available for U.S. personnel involved with future training iterations (Quarters are available for future events with only minimal restoration)	
Classrooms that effectively facilitate training	Maintain facilities and infrastructure for future training events	U.S. applies contractor support model that PN cannot carry forward	Build sustainment plan based on PN capabilities and culture	Facilities are available to PN for future courses	
Field areas that effectively facilitate training		—	—		
Equipment and facilities that are powered throughout the training cycle		—	—	The power grid remains in service for continued use	
Facilities that are managed to support training activities	—	—	—	—	—
IT equipment that effectively augments instruction	PN continues to utilize remaining IT systems or upgrades their existing systems	PN lacks absorptive capacity to use IT systems beyond U.S. provided training	PN officials open to continued engagement and follow-up actions	IT systems that facilitate training goals are maintained for future use	Phase core output 2, continuing maintenance and sustainment of new forces and equipment, training facilities, and materials

ment plan prior to facility turnover (or prior to facility construction) that is based on PN capabilities and culture.

Facilities: Outcomes

The subordinate outcome of this line of effort is *facilities that provide a secure environment for U.S. and PN personnel and that are conducive to meeting U.S. BPC goals*. The overall model outcomes are 2 (maintenance and sustainment occurring and training capability preserved) and 3 (relationships created or preserved such that further security cooperation is possible).

Curriculum and Training Content: Postengagement

Two activities in the postengagement phase pertain to the curriculum (Table 5.19). First, the *material used in the course should be provided to the students, with copies going to responsible government agencies,* if printed materials figured prominently in the course. Second, *PN officials should be consulted on whether they want to conduct the training again, modify the curriculum, or attempt to conduct it on their own with this or another curriculum.* These efforts lead to three subordinate outputs:

- an evolving curriculum that meets PN goals (the sufficient output is curriculum that can be built on for future events)
- the PN continuing to develop and use formal training materials (the sufficient output is that PN makes training processes more standardized)
- a partner military better suited to participating in international operations (the sufficient output is a PN military informed about requirements for participation in international operations).

The product of the postengagement curriculum is phase core output 2 (continuing maintenance and sustainment of new forces and equipment, training facilities, and materials).

Curriculum and Training Content: Outcomes

As stated previously, this line of effort addresses all three broad model outcomes (Table 5.20). Additionally, it has three subordinate outcomes:

- a curriculum that enables development of PN capabilities in line with U.S. and partner goals
- creation of a cadre of trained personnel within the PN's services
- a PN more receptive to opportunities for troop contributions.

Table 5.19
Logic Model: Postengagement Phase of the Curriculum and Training Content Category

Specific Inputs	Activities	Disrupters (Activities–Outputs)	Workarounds (Activities–Outputs)	Subordinate Outputs—Ideal (Sufficient)	Category Phase Outputs Contribute to . . .
Curriculum that has been verified as effective in achieving PN and U.S. goals	Engage PN counterparts to determine follow-on training requirements and level of U.S. involvement	Curriculum becomes outdated quickly; PN conditions and tasks change, and training does not remain applicable	Update curriculum with each training iteration	The curriculum evolves to meet PN goals (Curriculum can be built on for future events)	Phase core output 2, continuing maintenance and sustainment of new forces and equipment, training facilities, and materials
Training materials that effectively augment instruction	Materials provided to graduates and PN officials	Individuals do not retain manuals	Print manuals to be maintained by unit, headquarters, and ministry officials	PN maintains practice of developing and using formal training materials (PN makes training processes more standardized)	
Curriculum that has been verified as effective in achieving standards for international operations	—	—	—	PN military is better suited to participate in international operations (PN military informed of requirements for participation in international operations)	

Table 5.20
Logic Model: Outcomes of the Curriculum and Training Content Category

Subordinate Outcomes	Highest Level Outcome Category Contributed to . . .
Curriculum enables development of PN capabilities in line with U.S. and PN goals	1. Capacity is built: Capable units are formed and equipped in accordance with objectives
Cadre of trained personnel is created in PN service	
—	2. Capacity is sustained: Maintenance and sustainment are occurring, and a training capability has been preserved (or institutionalized)
PN more receptive to opportunities for troop contributions	3. The relationship with the PN continues: Relationships are created or preserved, making further security cooperation possible

Using the BPC Training and Equipping Logic Model as Part of an Assessment Framework

The logic model described in Chapters Two, Three, Four, and Five is central to the BPC assessment framework we propose. However, that framework needs to be tailored to specific BPC efforts and contexts. This chapter discusses a number of different ways in which the BPC training and equipping logic model can actually be *used*.

A logic model embodies the theory of change of a program or effort, the chain of logic that connects the resources provided and the activities conducted with the desired results produced and their effects. Using a logic model as part of an assessment framework allows the user to identify where the chain of logic might break or has broken. Breaks in the chain of logic could stem from some sort of execution failure (inputs not being provided, activities not being executed, or activities not being properly executed) or from some kind of disrupter or barrier that is preventing inputs from being transformed into outputs or keeping outputs from realizing intended outcomes. Once a break or potential break in the chain of logic has been identified, steps can be taken to find a correction, repair, or workaround.

Three Questions, Three Places to Start

Using the logic model as part of an assessment framework can help BPC planners or managers answer one or more of three questions. These questions depend on when in the BPC process assessment is being considered:

- Prior to execution, this framework could help planners answer the question: **What could go wrong with the planned BPC effort?**
- During BPC execution or delivery, this framework could help managers answer the questions: **Is everything going according to plan? If not, why not, and what can be done about it?**
- After BPC execution or delivery, this framework could help managers answer the questions: **Were all objectives achieved? If not, why not, and what can be done about it in the future (either in this context or elsewhere)?**

The entire logic model is in the Excel spreadsheet associated with this report. That matrix intentionally includes some redundancies and can be quite intimidating at first glance. We do *not* recommend that users attempt to populate the entire logic model as part of their assessment process. Instead, we encourage users to identify relevant chains of logic within the model to better focus assessment efforts on specific problem areas.

As Figure 2.3 illustrated, the logic model has both vertical and horizontal divisions. From top to bottom, the model is broken into ten input categories (listed in Chapter Two). The columns, from left to right, move through inputs, activities, outputs (including disrupters and workarounds) for each of the three temporal phases (pre-, during, and post-), ending on the right with overall outcomes.

Depending in part on when the logic model is being applied and in part on what assessors already know, there are at least three places to start and ways to use the logic model to identify future or past breaks in the chain of logic (and possible steps to repair them), as discussed in the following subsections.

Left to Right

One way to begin to use the logic model for assessment is to begin on the left, starting with the input categories, and trace nodes across until problems (or possible problems) are found.

To use this "begin at the beginning" approach, start with input categories that have been or might be problematic. When information is limited, ask subject-matter experts (SMEs) to identify possible problem areas. SME input being insufficient to ascertain the presence or extent of a problem indicates any area that might need more careful measurement and observation (further discussed below).

Following the logic model from left to right and identifying imperiled or unsatisfied nodes will show the possible consequences of such problems (by following the logic further to the right and seeing what could be affected), identify nodes needing additional observation or measurement (if assessors cannot determine *why* an input or output is absent or where a disrupter originates), and help identify possible solutions (either from candidate workarounds or using other problem-solving approaches).

For example, in one of our deep-dive case studies, early efforts to improve partner rotary-wing capabilities failed to produce appreciable results. A left-to-right assessment approach revealed that this should not have come as a surprise. Of the ten input categories in the logic model, five (U.S. political will, PN political will, funding, PN trainees, equipment to be trained on) contained significant deficiencies in individual inputs in the preengagement phase. That particular effort was doomed before it even got started.

Right to Left

Another way to begin to use the logic model without facing the entire matrix at once is to work backward, from right to left. Recall that the highest level outcomes are on the far right. If all outcomes are satisfactory, the chains of logic are being preserved, and little remedial assessment is required. However, if any of the ultimate outcomes are at all deficient (or otherwise unsatisfactory), working from right to left can help reveal why. Identify a deficient outcome to focus on. Begin by seeing which input categories support or contribute to that output. Then, work backward along the contributing input area rows, following the line of deficiency from right to left until the break in the chain (or just the extra friction in the system) is identified. If the first node back from right to left is fine, preliminarily conclude that that input category is making its contribution, and move down to one of the other input categories that contributes to the outcome of interest and trace it back. Eventually, one or more deficiencies (missing or deficient inputs, present disrupters, etc.) should be identified, after which remedial action can be considered, or focal nodes for additional data collection can be identified.

For example, in one of our case studies, one of the high-level outcomes (1, capacity built—capable units formed and equipped in accordance with objectives) was deficient; fewer units than expected had been formed over the course of the program. Working from right to left back along the chains of logic revealed no significant problems in postengagement core output; however, during engagement, core output 2 (required number of trainees complete the program and achieve certification) was found to be deficient, with matriculations from the program being below 50 percent of what was expected. Reviewing input categories connected with engagement outcome 2 showed that most were fine, with one glaring exception: PN trainees. Working backward along the trainee input category showed that a number of deficient inputs and disrupters were present. While a sufficient number of trainees had been identified and assigned to participate in training, a smaller number attended regularly, and a smaller number still successfully completed training. Lower-than-anticipated attendance stemmed from competing duties; the high OPTEMPO of PN forces limited the time they had available for training. Further, many of the trainees who did attend training were unmotivated, did not pay sufficient attention to the training, or were deficienct in baseline preparation for the training. Lower-than-expected trainee input coupled with lower-than-expected trainee output produced lower-than-expected overall outputs and outcomes.

Radiating Out from a Specific Node

A third way to employ the logic model might be to start with a specific node. This use is perhaps most likely when reports of a problem come in from the field (such as a missing or late input or the threat of a possible disrupter) but could also come from warning of a possible concern from a country SME during planning. Find the logic model node that best captures the concern or issue. There may not be an exact match, because the logic model's nodes are intentionally generic, but there should be something close enough. From there, work to the left and the right to see what friction or disruption in that node could affect. Consider making additional observations or collecting data not only on the node of concern but also on nodes to the left and right to provide warning (and details) of actual disruptions. Early awareness of a problem or possible problem should help identify opportunities for better monitoring of the situation and of possible solutions or workarounds, should the problem worsen.

For example, one of our cases involved a disrupter that developed during the engagement phase of a training exercise. U.S. officials were struggling with an inability to reach and engage with senior PN officials who were critical to the efforts to build capacity. To be sure, once supporting U.S. personnel and units were identified and informed choices had been made about which departments and levels to engage with (inputs), further engaging with PN personnel to conduct activities per the training plan was the next logical activity. When these individuals were unreachable, the country team and embassy staff took the step of alerting senior U.S. policymakers to see if they could raise the issue during higher-level interactions with their PN counterparts. Finding a specific problem node in the logic model enables an assessor to look earlier and see whether an input is missing or a disrupter exists prior to that node and, later, to see what outputs and outcomes are in jeopardy if the problem is not resolved.

Contextualizing the Logic Model

Whether working with the logic model left to right, right to left, starting with a specific node, or some other approach, there may still be a need to adapt the logic model to the specific context. The logic model as presented is broad, fairly comprehensive, and fairly generic. Many nodes likely correspond to contextual challenges that may not be of concern to a specific effort and can be safely ignored. Similarly, some generic nodes could benefit from more precision in a specific context. Consider, for example, the disrupter *lack of trainee attention (distracted, high, fatigued, unauthorized absence, etc.)*. If this disrupter is present, it is likely that one of the listed reasons for deficient trainee attention is paramount, and it is useful to know which it is. For example, if drug addiction is a major problem in the PN military and is the source of the problem, it may be worth modifying the logic model to explicitly specify that.

Similarly, the context may require adding additional disrupters (or making disrupters more specific) based on previous experience in the country or with similar efforts. Further, if the specific BPC effort or program has distinctive inputs, activities, or outputs that are part of its essential logic but not well covered by the baseline model, these should be added. The BPC training and equipping logic model presented in Chapters Two, Three, Four, and Five is extensive and fairly generic and should cover most of the main logical steps in most training and/or equipping oriented BPC, but it is not universal and so may require some adjustment or addition of specificity to match to a particular effort.

The Logic Model Helps with Selection and Prioritization of Measures

A logic model like the one presented here encapsulates a theory of change and, done well, suggests things to measure. Each layer in the logic model suggests clear measures. One might ask such questions as the following:

- Were all the resources needed for the effort available? (inputs)
- Were all activities conducted as planned? On schedule? (activities)
- Did the activities produce what was intended? How many personnel completed the program of instruction satisfactorily? (outputs).

These questions point directly to possible measures and also help prioritization. Not everything needs to be measured in great detail or particularly emphasized in data collection. For example, the level of assessment data collection for inputs may be quick, simple, and qualitative: "Were all the resources needed for this effort available?" "Yes." (Were the answer "No," some relatively simply follow-up questions about which resources were lacking would follow, but the exact amounts of the deficiencies would still not be all that relevant.)

Qualitative Stoplight Assessment

When making initial use of the BPC training and equipping logic model, whether working left to right, right to left, or otherwise, we suggest beginning with qualitative categorical SME "stoplight" assessments. In our experimentation with and validation of the logic model on the four empirical cases, we actually discovered that it was best to use a four-part stoplight (red, yellow, green, and then the addition of orange). In initial scoring, we found too much use of yellow; it had became a very broad, catchall category. Where red denoted serious deficiency and green denoted sufficiency, yellow ended up covering everything from "tolerable but not that strong" all the way to "bad, but not wholly disruptive." The addition of orange subsumed the worse half of what was previously yellow and left us with the following scale:

- green—good/sufficient; marginal improvement may be possible, but not necessary
- yellow—adequate but marginal; improvement possible, but not necessary
- orange—bad, but short of wholly disruptive; improvement recommended
- red—highly or wholly disruptive; continuing on the logic path past a red node impossible or highly inefficient; improvement required.

When using the BPC training and equipping logic model, all preliminary assessments should be made at this categorical stoplight measurement level. SME consultation or "BOGSAT" with trainers, program managers, and/or country team members should be sufficient. From that preliminary assessment, nodes for which more precision is required or desired should become apparent.

While Qualitative Assessment Is Sufficient for Many Nodes, Some Require Greater Precision

As noted, for the vast majority of nodes, qualitative categorical, stoplight assessment is sufficient. For example, if delivery of equipment to be trained on is red because the equipment was not delivered prior to the scheduled beginning of training, it is not particularly important to know exactly how many days the delivery was late. Knowing that gear was not present for training is sufficient to understanding why training failed to meet equipment-related objectives. Understanding *why* the delivery was late is much more important than any precise quantitative measurement of lateness. Reaching such an understanding may require further inquiry, but that would be narrative inquiry, not something requiring further detailed measurement.

Initial qualitative assessment, however, may well reveal additional things to observe or understand at the holistic level and may also reveal things that need to be tracked with great precision (things should result in a count, or a frequency). In fact, a few things should always be measured more precisely. Even if a program or effort goes perfectly (leaving no room for assessment to support improvement and suggesting that managers should simply "stay the course"), some things should still be measured for accounting and accountability purposes. These things include accounting-type measures (funds expended, equipment delivered) and throughput measures, efficiency, outputs, and outcomes. While some of these things are fairly straightforward to measure if measurement is planned for (number of trainees arriving for training, number of trainees completing training), some things, such as proficiency or trained troops or readiness of trained formations, are harder to measure.

Getting to More-Precise Measurement

As noted in the previous section, when using a logic model as a foundation for conducting assessment, a surprisingly large number of the things that need to be measured can be satisfactorily scored at the categorical, stoplight level based on SME input. Awareness that a critical node is red is often sufficient to start fixing it; an exact quantification of how red is not all that useful. For example, if the disrupter *lack of trainee attention (distracted, high, fatigued, unauthorized absence, etc.)* is present and given a red stoplight score based on trainer input, knowing exactly what percentage of trainees have this problem is less useful than knowing, first, that it is a significant problem (and would only be given a red stoplight if it were) and, second, which category or categories of lack of attention are in play (intoxication, fatigue, something else). Once there is a clear qualitative understanding of the problem, progress toward a solution is possible without any more-specific measurement.

However, for certain logic model nodes, more-precise measurement provides additional benefits. For example, a training completion rate is a useful overall measure of training efficiency and requires only two measures to calculate: number of trainees beginning training and number of trainees satisfactorily completing training. Further, both counts are useful for accounting (and accountability) purposes in their own right. If the training completion rate is low, the specific reasons trainees are not completing training become interesting. However, circumstances will dictate whether the reasons need to be precisely quantified or whether a qualitative assessment will be sufficient. If trainers provide the information that most failures to complete are due to trainees going AWOL prior to completion because of extended time away from their families, the precise breakdown by individual of why trainees did not complete training provides little additional information at the cost of considerable additional work and record keeping.

In addition to needed precise quantitative measures for certain core inputs and outputs (amounts of equipment delivered, trainees entering training, trainees completing training), a good BPC assessment effort would also attempt some measurement of the proficiency of troops completing training and perhaps of proficiency at the unit level (depending on the intended level of the training or exercise). While a stoplight assessment might be sufficient here, too, most contexts will require something more rigorous and consistent than a SME's qualitative stoplight assessment. Ideally, assessments of proficiency would have several features: They would be consistent, so that they could be applied equally and measure accurately and comparably across different individuals and formations (in the measurement literature, this is called reliability),[1] and there should also be some clear and consistent minimum threshold for a passing assessment, a standard that indicates whether an individual or unit is certified as is "go" rather than "no go."

So, how should individual and collective proficiency measurements of the outputs of BPC be made? Where a measurement approach and standard (such as the certification standards for international peacekeeping) already exists, it should be used. Where none exists, one should be developed as part of BPC planning, and data should be collected to fulfill it. It is not necessary to reinvent the wheel. U.S. forces complete a wide range of types of training themselves and are assessed on their proficiency at both the individual and collective levels. While BPC efforts may not exactly duplicate all training tasks and while the desired standard for PN forces may not be as exacting as that for U.S. troops, the basic framework should align almost entirely. A detailed discussion of the various training assessment approaches available and used throughout DoD is beyond the scope of this report.

---

[1]   Colin Phelan and Julie Wren, "Exploring Reliability in Academic Assessment," web page, Cedar Falls, Iowa: University of Northern Iowa, Office of Academic Assessment, undated.

References

Babbitt, Eileen, Diana Chigas, and Robert Wilkinson, *Theories and Indicators of Change: Concepts and Primers for Conflict Management and Mitigation*, Washington, D.C.: U.S. Agency for International Development, 2013.

DeShazo, Peter, Tanya Primiani, and Philip McLean, "Back from the Brink: Evaluating Progress in Colombia, 1999–2007," Washington, D.C.: Center for Strategic and International Studies, November 2007. As of December 18, 2014:
http://csis.org/files/media/csis/pubs/071112-backfromthebrink-web.pdf

Drake, Bruce, "Curbing Military Aid to Egypt Has Support Among the U.S. Public," Washington, D.C.: Pew Research Center, October 9, 2013. As of December 18, 2014:
http://www.pewresearch.org/fact-tank/2013/10/09/
curbing-military-aid-to-egypt-has-support-among-the-u-s-public/

Felbab-Brown, Vanda, *Shooting Up: Counterinsurgency and the War on Drugs*, Washington D.C.: Brookings Institution Press, 2009.

Jane's Information Group, "Romania, Armed Forces," *Jane's Country and Military Assessments*, November 7, 2002.

Jane's Information Group, "Procurement: Senegal," *Jane's Military and Security Assessments*, October 13, 2011.

Joint Chiefs of Staff, *Commander's Handbook for Assessment Planning and Execution*, Vers. 1.0, Suffolk, Va.: J-7, Joint and Coalition Warfighting, September 9, 2011. As of September 20, 2012:
http://www.dtic.mil/doctrine/doctrine/jwfc/assessment_hbk.pdf

Mertens, Donna M., and Amy T. Wilson, *Program Evaluation Theory and Practice: A Comprehensive Guide*, New York, N.Y.: The Guilford Press, 2012.

Moroney, Jennifer D. P., David E. Thaler, and Joe Hogler, *Review of Security Cooperation Mechanisms Combatant Commands Utilize to Build Partner Capacity*, Santa Monica, Calif.: RAND Corporation, RR-413-OSD, 2013. As of December 18, 2014:
http://www.rand.org/pubs/research_reports/RR413.html

Mozena, Dan, U.S. Ambassador to Bangladesh, "America's Partnership with Bangladesh National Defense College Mirpur," remarks, Dhaka, Bangladesh: Embassy of the United States of America, August 5, 2013.

Nixon, Michael, Heather Peterson, Beth Grill, and Jessica Yeats, *The RAND Security Cooperation Prioritization and Propensity Matching Tool*, Santa Monica, Calif.: RAND Corporation, TL-112-OSD, 2013. As of December 9, 2014:
http://www.rand.org/pubs/tools/TL112.html

Osburg, Jan, Christopher Paul, Lisa Saum-Manning, Dan Madden, and Leslie Adrienne Payne, *Assessing Locally Focused Stability Operations*, RR-387-A, 2014.

Paul, Christopher, "Foundations for Assessment: The Hierarchy of Evaluation and the Importance of Articulating a Theory of Change," *Small Wars Journal*, Vol. 10, No. 3, 2014.

Paul, Christopher, Colin P. Clarke, Beth Grill, Stephanie Young, Jennifer D. P. Moroney, Joe Hogler, and Christine Leah, *What Works Best When Building Partner Capacity and Under What Circumstances?* Santa Monica, Calif.: RAND Corporation, MG-1253/1-OSD, 2013. As of December 9, 2014:
http://www.rand.org/pubs/monographs/MG1253z1.html

Paul, Christopher, Jennifer D. P. Moroney, Beth Grill, Colin P. Clarke, Lisa Saum-Manning, Heather Peterson, Brian Gordon, *What Works Best When Building Partner Capacity in Challenging Contexts?* Santa Monica, Calif.: RAND Corporation, RR-937-OSD, forthcoming.

Paul, Christopher, Jessica M. Yeats, Colin P. Clarke, and Miriam Mathews, *Assessing and Evaluating Efforts to Inform, Influence, and Persuade: Desk Reference*, Santa Monica, Calif.: RAND Corporation, RR-809/1-OSD, 2015. As of June 17, 2015:
http://www.rand.org/pubs/research_reports/RR809z1.html

Phelan, Colin, and Julie Wren, "Exploring Reliability in Academic Assessment," web page, Cedar Falls, Iowa: University of Northern Iowa, Office of Academic Assessment, undated. As of April 7, 2014:
http://www.uni.edu/chfasoa/reliabilityandvalidity.htm

Project on Middle East Democracy, "Working Group on Egypt Releases Letter to President Obama," February 3, 2014. As of Febraury 5, 2015:
http://pomed.org/homepage-entries/working-group-on-egypt-letter-to-the-president/

Pubby, Manu, "Indo-US Exercise: Antony Wary of Political Fallout," *Indian Express*, September 6, 2011.

"Regionally Aligned Forces and Global Engagement," presented to the Contemporary Military Forum III , 2013 AUSA Conference, October 18, 2013. As of February 5, 2015:
https://www.ausa.org/meetings/2013/AnnualMeeting/Documents/Presentation_RegionallyAlignedForcesAnd%20Global%20Engagement.pdf

Rossi, Peter H., Mark W. Lipsey, Howard E. Freeman, *Evaluation: A Systematic Approach*, Thousand Oaks, Calif.: Sage Publications, 2004.

Sharp, Jeremy M., "Egypt: Background and U.S. Relations," Congressional Research Service, June 5, 2014. As of January 6, 2015:
http://fas.org/sgp/crs/mideast/RL33003.pdf

Stern, Lewis M., "Diverging Roads: 21st Century U.S.-Thai Defense Relations," *Strategic Forum*, No. 241, June 2009.

U.S. Government Accountability Office, *Palestinian Authority: U.S. Assistance Is Training and Equipping Security Forces, but the Program Needs to Measure Progress and Faces Logistical Constraints*, Washington, D.C., GAO-10-505, May 2010.

U.S. Senate, Committee on Armed Services, *The Findings of the Iraqi Security Forces Independent Assessment Commission*, 110th Cong., 1st Sess., September 6, 2007.

Zanotti, Jim, "U.S. Security Assistance to the Palestinian Authority," Washington, D.C.: Congressional Research Service, January 2010.